LIFE *artist*

Scrapbooking Life's Journey **BY ALI EDWARDS**

CREATING

Keepsakes

SCRAPBOOK MAGAZINE

Keepsakes
SCRAPBOOK MAGAZINE

FOUNDING EDITOR Lisa Bearnson

EDITOR-IN-CHIEF Brian Tippetts

CREATIVE EDITOR Britney Mellen

SENIOR WRITER Rachel Thomae

SENIOR EDITOR Vanessa Hoy

COPY EDITOR Kim Sandoval

EDITORIAL ASSISTANTS Joannie McBride, Fred Brewer, Liesl Russell

ART DIRECTOR, SPECIAL PROJECTS Erin Bayless

PRODUCTION DIRECTOR Tom Stuber

SENIOR PRODUCTION DIRECTOR Terry Boyer

ADVERTISING MANAGER Becky Lowder

ADVERTISING COORDINATOR Janel Donner

SALES SUPPORT Kristin Schaefer

ADVERTISING SALES Debbie Downs, 801/583-1043
                   Barbara Tanner, 801/942-6080

ADVERTISING SALES, ONLINE/INTERACTIVE Sherrie Bratke, 801/495-7231

DISTRIBUTOR & NATIONAL ACCOUNTS Tara Green, 801/413-9784

RETAIL SALES MANAGER LaRita Godfrey

INDEPENDENT STORES Becky Cude, 801/816-8337
                    Claudia Mann, 801/816-8366

CK MEDIA

CHIEF EXECUTIVE OFFICER David O'Neil

CREATIVE DIRECTOR Lin Sorenson

CHIEF FINANCIAL OFFICER/CHIEF OPERATING OFFICER Rich Fankhauser

VP/CONSUMER MARKETING DIRECTOR Susan DuBois

DIRECTOR OF EVENTS Paula Kraemer

GROUP PUBLISHER/QUILTING Tina Battock

VP/ONLINE DIRECTOR Chad Phelps

editor's note

I WILL NEVER FORGET THE DAY I MET Ali Edwards. In 2004, the CK editorial staff got together for a meeting—a creative retreat of sorts at Thanksgiving Point in Utah. Ali was relaxed. She was happy. I had only just met her, but I felt so comfortable around her, and we quickly became friends.

Ali has a casual grace about her that can take her from high heels to flip-flops with ease. She's just as comfortable speaking at a convention in front of hundreds of new faces as she is on the couch, relaxing and playing with her darling boy, Simon.

It makes sense then, that Ali scrapbooks the same way she lives her life. She manages to capture everyday life in beautiful works of art that could exist just as seamlessly in a prestigious art gallery as they could on a coffee table in the living room. And that, right there, is what makes Ali such an inspiration.

While some artists in high esteem would strive to display their work in the loftiest exhibit, Ali would take you to her favorite café in Oregon and give you a personal tour of her albums—albums that beg to be touched. Albums that share memories captured in a way that allows others to experience them vicariously.

And experience them you will. I experienced this firsthand when I saw Ali's "One Year" album collection (on page 126). I immediately wanted to pick up the delightful little box and explore each minature book inside. I was instantly inspired to create something equally "touchable" for my own home: a little suitcase of photos and memories for my toddler son to enjoy and treasure.

I know you'll experience the same inspiration on the pages of this book. Let Ali help you capture your life in a way that resonates with you, then go and turn those memories into something for your own coffee table. Something that family members and guests will linger over—something that will become tangible evidence of the life you live and the memories you love. Before you know it, you'll be creating your very own "life art."

Brithey Mellen

What a glorious spring day. We spent the first warm Saturday of 2007 at Liberty Park picnicking and playing with the ducks and pigeons.

contents

scrapbooking
and life

GROWING UP, I NEVER CONSIDERED myself a creative person. I was more interested in academics and sports and boyfriends than in making stuff.

I began scrapbooking in 2002 as a way to deal with all the stuff that had been accumulating since my son's birth early that year. I had been hunting for a baby book—a cool, modern baby book in which to tell his story—and had been unsuccessful in that search.

So I turned to the Internet. There I first discovered modern scrapbooking. Enlarged photographs on layouts, designs that were aesthetically pleasing, lots of journaling—a whole new world presented itself to me on my computer. I suddenly knew that this was the approach I wanted to take with my son's baby photos and memorabilia.

What I quickly realized as I began buying stuff and creating was that I was in love. I was in love with all the cool papers and products and ideas ... but most of all, I was in love with this new-found expression of myself.

I was also totally in love with my new baby.

Having a baby was a total life change. Being at home with him forced me to slow down. To look at things in a new way. I was at a point in my life where I was open to growth.

I felt blessed and lucky to be able to be home with my son. I loved watching him grow—seeing the world through his new-born eyes. But at the same time, being a new mom was a lot harder than I ever imagined. Being all alone with an infant was exhausting and challenging and so very hard, both physically and emotionally.

Scrapbooking became my outlet. My way of dealing with all of the changes in my life. My way of dealing with my emotions. Through the photos I took, I was able to see (literally see) how really amazing and lucky and blessed I was. Scrapbooking helped me take a look at the life I was living. It helped me make changes that would positively affect my life experience.

Over the last few years, scrap-booking has become the way I've grown to know myself. To stretch myself. To express my thoughts and feel-ings. Scrapbooking combines my love of writing and photography and design and allows me to tell my stories in creative ways. I create because it fills me up inside.

This book is about scrapbooking and about life. About capturing the life you're living, have lived and will live. About creating art from the photographs, words, documents and bits of this and that…those things that help tell the stories of who you really are.

When I wrote this book, my goal was to create the sort of book that I love to read: one that both inspires and motivates. As you read this book, I want you to feel the overwhelming desire to create something. To upload some photos, to paint a canvas, to jot down a few notes, to make a layout, to try a challenge, to tell a story.

To capture life, to create art.

Edwards

life artist notes

"Art is life, life is life, but to lead life artistically is the art of life." —Peter Altenberg

I'M OFTEN ASKED HOW THIS WHOLE "LIFE ARTIST" thing began, and here's the story.

For the last couple of years, I've been feeling that the term "scrapbooker" doesn't completely fit me or what I do. I'm more than the image the term conjures in the minds of those who only experience scrapbooking as cutting up photographs and decorating pages with cute little bunny rabbit stickers (no offense to bunny rabbits or stickers; I happen to quite enjoy both!)

I wanted something that was more reflective of who I am and how I create. Sometimes I create perfectly aligned layouts that are measured with the greatest of care. Other times, I throw down paint and express myself in an entirely different manner.

The term "life art" came to me on an airplane. I do a lot of flying these days from one event to another, which provides me with lots of quiet time to think. On January 20, 2006, I was flying from Oregon to Virginia, and it all started to come together for me. I grabbed a pen and started making notes. I wrote and wrote and underlined and got all excited about a whole new definition for this awesome thing I get to do, to be.

A life artist, most simply, is someone who captures life and creates art.

The life art philosophy continued to evolve as I taught workshops near and far. It started to grow through phrases I found myself repeating over and over again, like: "It is OK." "Embrace imperfection." "Don't make it more complicated than it has to be."

So much of being a life artist is about attitude. About how you feel about yourself and what you create. It's choosing to be open to all the wonderful possibilities in creating art that celebrates the life we are living.

This certainly doesn't mean that all art created by life artists is wonderfully happy. Life artists recognize that life consists of both good and bad, that our experiences are a sum of who we really are, that there is beauty in sharing authentic stories, even the so-called "imperfect ones."

Why life art? Because what we do is so much more than just celebrating birthdays or scrapbooking holidays. Most of us began at that point—I know I did. But along the way, I've discovered that scrapbooking is more. It's personal. It's about opening up and sharing your own life. It makes us human. It makes us reflect on who we are and where we want to be in

life. It helps us discover the beauty (the art) in the midst of our life, and the life in the midst of our art.

Life art is limitless. If you are open, it can take you to places you never would have imagined (even if that place is just within yourself.)

Life Art Principles

It's about being awake.

It means celebrating everyday things.

It means letting go of your need for perfection.

It means using words and photos to tell your story.

It means sharing yourself.

It's about being real.

It's about documenting, telling, celebrating and experiencing life.

It's about being open and embracing the process of creativity.

It's about cultivating a lifestyle of creativity and beauty—with you as the creative director.

IT IS
OK
re·mem·ber (ri-mem'bẽr), v.t. [ME. remembren; OFr. remembrer, se remember < LL. rememorare, L. re-, back, again + memorare, to bring to remembrance < memor, mindful; cf. MEMORY], 1. to have (an event, thing, person, etc.) come to mind again; think of again: as, he suddenly remembered an appointment. 2. to bring back to mind by an effort; recollect; recall: as, he tried to remember the name. 3. to bear in mind; keep in the memory; be careful not to forget. 4. to keep (a person) in mind with some feeling, as of pleasure, gratitude, etc. 5. a) to keep (a person) in mind for a present, legacy, etc. b) to give a present or tip
FRONT NECK AND ARMHOLE FACING
3450
DOS
ATRAS

it is ok

MY NUMBER-ONE GUIDING CREATIVE PHILOSOPHY IS THE PHRASE, "IT IS OK."

"It is OK" is pretty much the answer to anything related to life art and creativity.

Over the last few years, as I've met and taught students all over the world, I've found myself saying over and over to them (as well as to myself), "It is OK."

It's OK to tell stories out of order; it's OK to do things just the way you want to do them; it's OK to journal a lot on some pages and write almost nothing on others. It's OK to feel the pressure of a crazy life and take some time for yourself to find balance. It's OK to take time just for you to play and create and tell your personal story.

"It is OK" is a philosophy of creating with perspective. It's an under-standing that your family is going to love what you make, no matter what. They're going to love that you took the time to tell a story, to use your own handwriting, to chronicle your own life as well as theirs.

"It is OK" is an attitude. It's looking at the things you're creating and giving yourself the chance to be happy, to accept and love what you create.

"It is OK" is rule-free. It's OK to create in a messy space or a clean one. It's OK to create simple pages or complex ones.

Whatever you're worried about related to creativity, the answer is . . . it is OK.

Now let's go find some of the questions . . .

... to **let go.**

"Life is the supreme creative act. We are always choosing, shaping, improvising, with what arises around us. The more we accept what is happening and let go of what we think should be happening or what we want to happen, the more free and alive we become." —Jennifer Louden

a hike

The concept of "It is OK"

is a tough one for many people. It's letting go of preconceived notions. It's letting go of the strict rules you've been taught. It's letting go of the need for perfection.

Creating stuff is inherently imperfect—it's a perfect parallel to life. Why stress yourself out over something that's innately beautiful in its imperfection? Embracing imperfection doesn't mean you don't care about how something turns out—it simply means that you let go of your personal need to control the outcome.

It you ever feel like you're being suffocated by your hobby, you're probably holding on too tight.

It is OK to . . .

Let go of the feeling that there's a right or wrong in what you're doing.

Let go of feeling like you need to have a specific style.

Let go of thinking that you either have to have all moments photos or all events photos.

Let go of the need to scrapbook in any sort of order.

Let go of the thought that you are not creative.

... *to create based on* *what* **inspires you** *at the moment.*

I create based on what's inspiring me at the moment.

This has been my method of scrapbooking from the beginning. I'm much more interested in telling stories I'm feeling excited about or compelled to tell. Where's the fun in creating based on a strict timeline? Where's the fun in scrapbooking because you feel like you must? Where's the creative joy in telling stories because you feel it's expected of you?

I'm in this hobby for the long run. It's a huge part of my everyday life, and I plan to enjoy the process.

Q: *How do you get to the point where being creative becomes part of your life?*

Just wake up. It can be as simple as this if you allow yourself. Wake up tomorrow and decide you're no longer going to question your ability to tell your own stories and your family's stories in your own creative voice. Just make the decision and go for it. This is the first step.

You're going to need to continue to remind yourself of this choice, because it's a choice you'll need to make every day until you come to the day when you wake up and don't need to tell yourself any more because it's just become a part of who you are. Each day I take a bit of time, even just a couple of minutes, and ask myself, "What's inspiring me at the moment, and what stories do I feel compelled to tell?"

beautiful glass bottles in all shapes + sizes

i always notice things in quantity... sheer #'s

Scrapbookers often ask me,

"Where do you begin your layouts? What is your process for creating a layout?"

My answer is simple: I always start by answering the question,

"What is the story I want to tell?" As soon as I understand the story, the question becomes, "How can I tell the story visually on this page or within this album?"

What's most important on my layout at right? For me, it's the photo and the story. When I began this page, I had four photos sitting on top of two sheets of brown cardstock. I looked at it for a bit, thought about the story I wanted to tell, looked at the products in my supply stash and made the decision to choose just one photo that best illustrated the story I wanted to tell in my journaling.

I adhered the photo and the patterned pieces directly to the chipboard file-folder pieces, cut around the edges with an X-acto knife and sanded around the outside to smooth the edges. Then I added a piece of patterned paper over the brown cardstock. But you know what? It was just too much. I love the simple page that resulted from feeling that it was OK to simply tell a story with words and photos.

Q: *I often feel paralyzed by all the cool products I own. I tend to hoard them, waiting for the perfect moment and place to use them. Any suggestions on how to just dig in and use what I have?*

This is a hurdle for so many scrapbookers. The old adage "too much of a good thing" applies here.

I've had the same experience (*and most likely will again*). The easiest way to work through it for me? Get to work making stuff. Give yourself permission to use that holy-grail product—pull it out of hiding and make something. Give yourself an assignment (or a series of assignments). Participate in challenges.

Tell yourself that it's really OK. It's OK to use those awesome products you've been collecting. And it's OK to not feel like you need to buy all of the latest and greatest all the time. Part of being a creative person is working with what you have and making use of all those cool products you fell in love with enough to buy. I can guarantee you there will always be more.

Another thing I've found helpful is to go through my supplies regularly. If there are items I don't love anymore, I donate them. The process of sifting through everything helps me remember what I do have and reignites all kinds of great creative urges.

IT IS OK ... to **redefine** the meaning of a "scrapbook page."

Do you love 12" x 12" layouts? Or 8½" x 11"? Or mini books?

It's OK to love all or one or a little bit of both. Don't let any of these choices force you to think too hard when it's time to create.

There's so much more to life art than just traditional scrapbook pages. The possibilities of telling your stories are endless.

If there's one thing I've learned over the past few years, it's that scrapbooking doesn't just mean creating layouts that fit into a 12" x 12" album.

Mini books and other projects are just as important to me as regular-sized scrapbooks.

My albums are non-chronological. They're based on themes, on stories that are continually being told.

For example, this is a political album that includes lots of different things: layouts; important papers that my husband, Chris, brings home; newspaper clippings; letters and more. It's a home for all of that content, all of that documentation, all of the information. It's my effort to tell a more complete story about my husband's political career.

What's different about this album from what you may have seen before is that it combines different sizes and shapes of page protectors. I didn't limit myself to any particular size or style. This was a really huge breakthrough for me.

I'm getting more and more passionate about this method all the time. It turns my scrapbook into a *life book*. This is an album that's alive. It's growing over time. It's not one I can sit down and complete in one day because the story is still evolving.

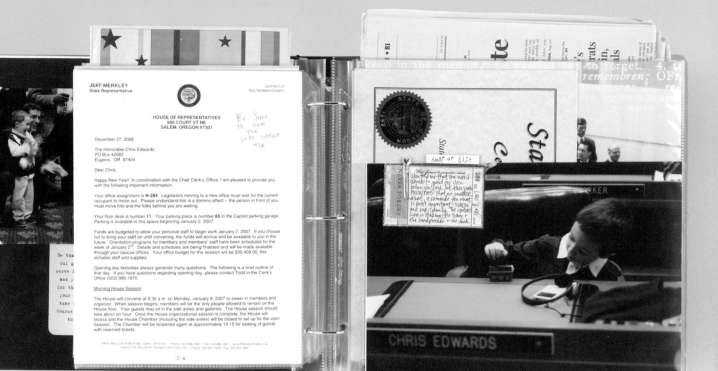

... to *live* with *your art*.

This is an old Kodak film pack I picked up at a local flea market. I'm continually on the hunt for interesting bits and pieces of used things that can become a part of the living art in my home. Treasures like this are a fantastic vehicle for displaying your own art in a way that speaks of both your creativity and your love for family.

Living with your own art is very fulfilling.

My home is filled with bits and pieces of our lives on the walls—mostly photographs with white mats in black frames. It's affirming to me as a creative person. It inspires and reminds me every day of who I love and what I value most. And I don't just enlarge the typical family photographs—I enlarge and frame everyday photographs that express a lot of emotion in their imperfection.

It's also OK to frame those layouts that have special meaning or significance to you, like the layout at left of my family enjoying swim activities. I have plans to put this layout in a frame and feature it in my home. Your layouts are your life art—put them on display just like you would a favorite painting or wall canvas.

... to **use what you have** on hand.

This mini book is a great example of a project where I really wanted to document lots of details, *like the cost of the land, the cost of the supplies to build our house and so on.*

That's the kind of stuff I think would be fascinating to look back on down the road. I also wanted to make sure the journaling reflected both the facts and the heart of what this house meant to us. But as I began gathering materials, it was clear I couldn't find everything I wanted to include. Ever had that happen? Such a bummer. But rather than spending time being grumpy about what I didn't have (or letting it stifle my creativity), I decided to be OK with what I did have and move forward with the album.

For this project, I had a mixture of photos on hand. Some were 4" x 6" and others were 5" x 7", and as you see here, I found a way to make it all work together. It was OK.

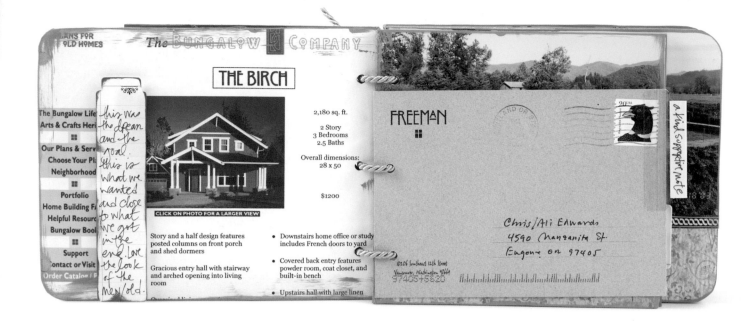

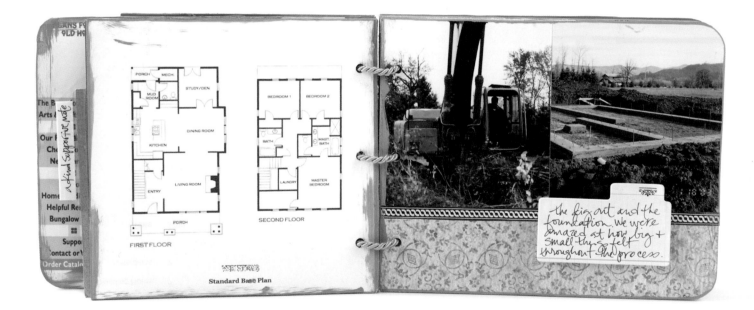

Album Tips

❶ I covered the chipboard title letters with a photograph for an artistic twist. It wasn't easy, and I'm not sure I would do it again. But it was still cool to try, and I like the finished look. (To try this technique: Turn your photo upside down and adhere each letter to the back of the photo, making sure the letters are aligned right side up with the photo. Use a craft knife to cut around each letter. Sand the edges to finish.)

❷ Don't ever feel confined to the way a certain product is presented. I began working with this Maya Road chipboard book and ended up taking it all apart, punching holes and turning it into a book with rings. I also used a craft knife to cut some of the pages down to be shorter than the others.

❸ Use paint as a layering tool to downplay a certain element. After adhering a map to the cover of the book, I felt it was too bright. I added a thin layer of paint over the map, which gave it a softer, more muted look.

... to repeat *what works for you.*

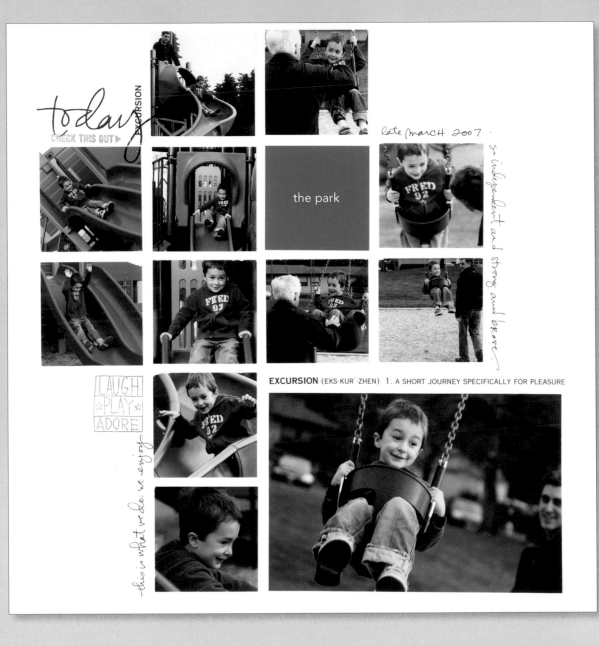

today

CHECK THIS OUT ▶

EXCURSION

the park

late march 2007

independent and strong and brave.

LAUGH
PLAY
ADORE

this is what we do: we enjoy.

EXCURSION (EKS·KUR´·ZHEN) 1. A SHORT JOURNEY SPECIFICALLY FOR PLEASURE

SO VERY SIMON

FALL 2006

CLASSIC

Q: *Just how do you dream up new page layouts? I struggle with new ideas and find that I keep placing things the same way on my pages.*

I'm actually OK with placing things the same way. When I complete something I love, I make a note of it so I can repeat it again on another project. It often feels like there's this presumed pressure to make something new every time you sit down to create. Where in the heck did that come from? If there's something that works for you and makes you feel confident creatively, then do it again. Do it on every project you want. Make it an everyday part of your personal process. Don't get hung up on trying to reinvent the wheel all the time.

The truth is that, down the road, no one will ever care that some of my layouts are the same design. In fact, they probably won't even notice. The photos will be different. The accents will be different. The stories will be different. It is OK.

What do I repeat over and over again? What works for me?

Cutting up photos. Enlarging photos. Word stickers, square and circle punches, linear page organization. Everyday themes.

I'd have to say that word stickers are probably my number-one favorite product. The reason? They're terrific for telling parts of my stories. They're simple. They look classy. They're *quick*. And I use them all the time.

As for techniques, one of my favorites continues to be using a square punch to crop my photos. I love that it allows me to get lots of images into a design to better tell a story. I'll continue to use the square punch on my pages until I'm tired of it and ready to try something different. And I love that I know I can always come back to it and count on it to do the job I want it to do.

... to **accept** that you are a *creative person.*

You are a creative person—there is no one else exactly like you.

It is OK to create in a way that reflects who you are at this moment in time.

It is OK for your creative process to stay the same or to change over the years.

It is OK to be yourself on your scrapbook pages.

It is OK to do the things you love in your art.

It is OK to define the word "creative" however you'd like.

DO THIS:

Write *"I am creative"* or *"I am an artist"* on a Post-it note and stick it someplace where you'll see it every day. My friend, Jeffrey, likes to place Post-its on his bathroom mirror to showcase his goals. Love that idea for goals, and I love it as a reminder that you are a unique individual and a creative being (maybe put up more than one Post-it note . . . these reminders are important!).

go with the flow

"GO WITH THE FLOW" MEANS A COUPLE OF DIFFERENT THINGS TO ME.

First and foremost, flow is about finding your groove, especially your creative flow—that "I'm so inspired, I have to make something right now" feeling. It's when you're fired up with excitement and overflowing with the desire to create. Man, I love that feeling. How do you get to that place? What do you need to do in order to get there? How can you set yourself up for success?

Second, flow means having the ability to adapt while you're creating (this would be "going with the flow"). It's a beautiful, organic notion that means being able to work around problems and issues that invariably come up while putting together mini books or layouts or other projects. It's about being flexible and knowing when to simply deal with a mistake and move on, and when to possibly begin again.

I tend to need chunks of time to find my flow. But, sometimes, I encounter something in my environment that's so super-powerful, I can feel the inspiration flowing through my veins. In the first part of this chapter, I'll share some of my favorite ways to find my groove (a.k.a. find the flow); in the second part, I'll tackle techniques for being able to adapt (a.k.a. go with the flow) while you're creating.

... *keep track* *of your cool ideas.*

GO WITH THE FLOW

I'm a visual learner. I need to see things first and then read for clarification.

Flow for me tends to come after I see or experience something. Often times it comes from looking through magazines or browsing online. I'm a collector of visual delights.

Since I'm constantly acquiring new visual stimuli, I've set up a great little system for myself. When I first encounter something (such as a cool page from a magazine), I add it to my bulletin board that hangs just above my computer desk. It remains there until I can't fit anything else on my bulletin board or until it just isn't fresh anymore. At that point, I'll move it into my "bits of inspiration" notebook, which is simply a compilation of visual delights. No real organization, just something I can easily reach for when I need a creative jolt.

I've tried setting up a big system for storing inspiring ideas in the past and it became more of a barrier to creativity than a generator. I spent more time organizing than I did creating. Go for simple.

Q: *Is your brain working all the time on new ideas? How do you remember all of them?*

My brain is working all the time in one way or another (and, seriously, this can be good and bad). Because I'm very visually oriented, I'm attracted to (or distracted by) things I see in my environment, especially words, fonts and the way things visually come together.

The only way I've found to hold on to these ideas is to write them down. I have journals/sketch books/notebooks around my house, and I also have a file set up on my computer just for storing ideas and inspiration. Keeping track of these brainstorms helps me when I'm not feeling in my groove, when my flow is off. It brings me back to things I've seen and the stories I want to tell.

My notes include layout ideas, topics for mini books, stories (conversations as well as documentation), concepts I want to investigate and things I want to remember. It's one of the main ways I capture life.

Sketchbooks are meant to be perfectly imperfect. They exist to let you regularly collect your thoughts and ideas so you can use them as jumping-off points when you need them. The key word here is *regularly*. Meaning often. There's a huge benefit in opening yourself up to this sort of practice because it will simply make you more aware of moments, your surroundings, your daily thoughts.

Whatever you put in your sketchbook is OK. You have permission to add whatever you want. Cut up stuff and stick it in there. Paint. Test out pens and inks and stamps in there. This isn't something for others. This is for you—for your own personal documentation.

If you've tried this in the past and it didn't work, try it again. Leading a creative lifestyle is a choice. You can choose to make this part of your everyday creative process. It takes very little time (you can do this in minutes a day!) and the rewards are wonderful.

I've loved magazines since I was a child. Even when I wanted to be a marine biologist and work with killer whales, I was still looking at magazines and feeling attracted to all the cool visual stuff. I used to tear out whole pages from fashion magazines and use them as wallpaper in my bedroom. Even then, I was attracted to things that were visually interesting—some simple and some complex.

Finding inspiration in magazines is quick and easy. It's a great way to get your flow going. And don't just turn to scrapbooking magazines. Check out design magazines, home-decorating magazines, lifestyle magazines, green-living magazines, photography magazines and even art magazines. Take a look at the flow of the articles and visuals, think about the topics presented, and examine the fonts and the headlines.

Figure out how you can incorporate an art technique into your own work. It doesn't have to be a major undertaking—start small; begin with a detail. Don't forget that you can also cut up those magazines and use the words and images on your projects as well.

Life-Art Challenge:
Both of the layouts on these pages were inspired by magazine advertisements. Creating them pushed me outside of my creative boundaries. I really like the white frames around the photographs. I usually scrapbook in a very linear way, so it was a challenge for me to create a layout where my photos weren't straight up and down (silly, but totally true).

Challenge yourself to find a magazine advertisement that speaks to you and create a layout based on it.

... schedule a **creativity field trip.**

Remember how cool field trips were when you were a little kid?

For me they were always a fantastic break from the same old, same old of the usual school routine (and an excuse to get out into the world).

These days, I still love field trips. They're one of my favorite ways to rejuvenate my creativity. Everyone needs to take a field trip once in a while; we all benefit from a change of scenery. It's a sure-fire way for me to find my flow.

Sometimes I head out on a field trip with something in mind. Other times, I go just for the purpose of motivating myself creatively. I leave my house with my mind open to the possibilities. The key for me is to just go.

Get in your car or on your bike or even use your own two feet and go somewhere new to you. It may be a new restaurant or a new store, or it may be simply walking down a new street in your neighborhood. The key is to get out from under your normal vision and see and experience something new.

I love doing this by myself, but you can also take along a friend, a partner or even your children. Kids are amazing at seeing what exists right in front of their noses, while we adults seem to have lost that ability.

One of my treasured field-trip locations is a local antique store

called Ruthie B's It's one of those awesome places where you have to work really hard to see everything because there's just so much stuff. Look up. Look down. Look in between the nooks and crannies and inside the chests of drawers that seem to be everywhere. So many treasures.

On my last visit, I was looking for something in particular. I had seen a photo on a blog featuring an old type-set drawer that the writer had converted into a piece of art. It brought back memories of my childhood because we had something similar in our hallway. In each of the little boxes, my mom had placed a memory, a piece of our lives. Knick knacks. This and that. Her version of life art. Now I have my own version in my own home: a photo-centric piece of art that showcases my family. I absolutely love how it turned out.

Life-Art Challenge:

Take yourself on a creativity field trip. Challenge yourself to find one thing that could be the starting point for a layout or a piece of life art (it doesn't have to be big or expensive). This challenge is really about the opportunity to live with your eyes open. There's so much inspiration right in front of us on a daily basis. Challenge yourself to begin noticing it.

... in a stack of **photos**.

Nothing gets me in the creative flow quite like a fresh stack of photos.

Most of my inspiration comes from my photos. I'm a photo-centric creator, which means I want my photos and words to be the center of each design I create. Going through a stack of photos stirs my emotions, conjures up already-forgotten moments and just gets me in the mood to make stuff.

For some people, stacks of photos can be overwhelming. They can be a sign of things not completed. Of layouts not created. Of being "behind" in their scrapbooking. A complete flow-stopper. But I think looking at stacks of photos should be exciting. Just think of all the cool stories in there waiting to be told. The life-art attitude is one of possibility. How cool is it to find those stories and know you can tell them in any way you like?

Change they way you view all of those stacks of photos.

One thing I've found as I thumb through a stack of photos is that stories come to me, feelings come to me, emotions come to me as I remember times, places, people and more. It can all come flooding back way too fast, making it easy to lose those feelings and moments all over again as you move from one photo to the next. It can feel like a tidal wave.

The answer is to slow down. Slow yourself down so you can really let yourself get to the heart of the matter.

Obviously, some stories are simple and sweet and silly, and others will require more in-depth thought before creating with them. My solution is to have paper and pen handy so I can track my thoughts and feelings as I'm investigating my photos. Don't be in a hurry, and don't let yourself get flooded. Pace yourself.

LOOK

REMINDER #71

SOMETIMES IT'S THE SMALL'ISH THINGS THAT TAKE UP THE MOST ROOM IN OUR HEARTS.

LIMITED EDITION

It would be super easy to simply pass by this photo without a second glance... OH but what you would miss. It's that **LOOK** when you know that i am watching you. It is a silly, "caught-in-the-act" kind of look. that is why i love this shot - taken from inside a store. ♥ you.

LITTLE TREASURES   BIG BOY

Life-Art Challenge:

Grab a stack of photos and a sheet of paper (or use this as a chance to begin a sketch book or book of lists). Go slowly through a stack of photos. Jot down notes of things that come to your mind as you look at each photo or group of photos. Pick one (yep, just one for now) and tell an underlying story about the photo—a story that may not be apparent on the surface, one that goes deeper than what you see at first glance. Create a layout based on that story.

I created the canvases here after watching Claudine Hellmuth's

DVD on beeswax collage. One canvas focuses on the story of a woman named Mary, while the other is a holiday decoration (I'm developing a great little collection of holiday life art). If you live in an area where class offerings are slim, check online or at a craft store for DVD/Internet class offerings. It's a whole new world.

Life-Art Challenge:

Check out the class offerings in your local area. Expand your horizons a bit or a lot. Even if you consider yourself primarily a scrapbooker, check out listings of local art, stamping, collage, book binding, computer, writing, photography and design classes in your area. All of these topics can help teach you how to tell your stories in new and unique ways. Your creative brain will benefit, and your flow will get a jump-start from being challenged. It can be scary to branch out, but it's oh-so worth it. Don't forget to look for online classes, too.

There's nothing quite like the positive energy that comes from a class environment to produce some of that sought-after flow. There's something powerful about the sharing that goes on, the creative vibes, the new ideas, the time away from your regular responsibilities.

As an instructor, I find that some of my most creative times have come just following a teaching event. It's there that I connect personally with people who share my passion for capturing life and creating art. It's there that I'm introduced to new concepts and ideas and products. It's there that I connect with people at the personal, individual level. I'm reminded over and over again of the many stories we have and how important it is to share those stories.

... *create* continuously.

One of the things I love most about this little book is that it sits on my desk.

It's out in the open and is constantly growing and changing. As I come across things during the day, I punch holes and add bits and pieces right into the binding. It's a simple, quick way to feel like you're doing something, recording something, documenting some part of your life as you experience it. It's a book that can grow and change right along with you. It's also a wonderful way to create in a continuous way, a way to go with the flow and record what's happening as it happens.

The supplies for this project are very basic. All you need are 4" x 6" alphabet index cards, metal rings and a hole punch. Just punch holes in the cards and in your photos and in anything else you want to include in your mini book. Make a cover if you'd like and then simply bind everything together with the metal rings.

The index cards do come in different sizes. I just went with the 4" x 6" size because I liked that they were the same size as my 4" x 6" photos. I can just punch holes in my extra photos and stick them right into this little book.

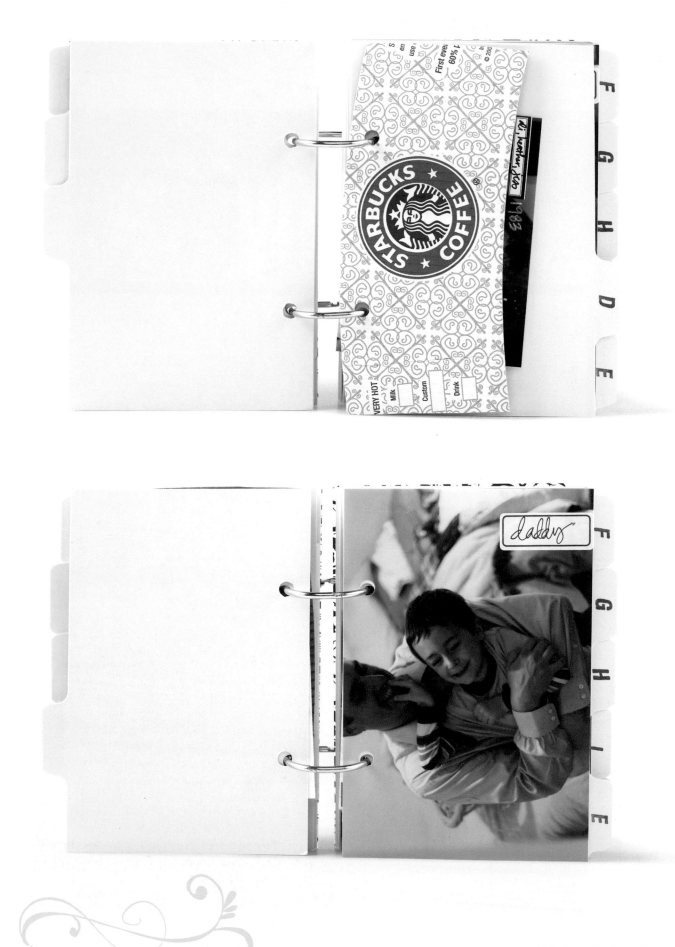

mEEting tHe GOV

write GOV

Thursday, 25 January 2007 at 09:34 AM

I grew up aware of politics. Interested at a distance. I could tell you who the President was and maybe a bit more than that about what was happening in the world. In college, after my failed attempt and realization that being a killer whale trainer at Sea World was probably not going to happen, I marched over to the English department and came up with my own major titled American Studies. If I wasn't going to be swimming with whales I might as well become an attorney (can you follow that logic?).

American Studies allowed me to focus on three main areas: American Literature, American History, and Political Science (with a bit of sociology thrown in for good measure). Loved it. It was all about reading and writing and culture and history and current events. It was at that time that I started paying a bit more attention. One of my favorite classes in college was called Politics and the Media. Loved learning about the dynamic between the two. That was back in 1996.

At no point did I ever really imagine I would be involved on a personal level.

Fast forward to this crazy last year. Politics and the workings of our state government are now a daily part of my life - at least from the stand point of asking a lot of questions each night when Chris comes home from the Capitol. I love hearing all about it and the crazy dynamics that go into government at this level.

Tuesday night I had the chance to go with Chris to the Governor's home (for those of you outside the US, the Governor is the leader of our state). We were invited, along with some of the other new legislators, for a small gathering to chat and talk politics and have a drink in a small group setting.

The kid in me was jumping for joy. Giddy is another good word.

After getting Simon all situated, we drove the short distance from the Capitol to the Governor's home which is called Mahonia Hall. When we got out of the car I had to make a decision: camera or no camera? I decided to leave the camera in the car. It felt intrusive and bulky and over-the-top. At the gate we were greeted by a security guard and then escorted to the door. We were lead into the house and seated in the living room where we met the Governor's wife Mary.

The other couple's arrived shortly after - there were four in all - and then the Governor arrived. It was interesting to be in his

home, the place he comes back to after a long day, after going from meeting to meeting, dealing with failures and successes, after speaking on the phone with two different families who lost sons in Iraq this week. It is also the house that other Governor's of the past have come home to (it was built in 1924 by Ellis F. Lawrence, the founder of the University of Oregon School of Architecture). I felt a really big sense of gratitude to him that he opened his home to us - making us welcome - I am sure that is all part of the job, but I felt comfortable and warm and welcomed.

I think that is something that will become even more interesting to me as time goes on, that line between public and private - between the person and the job. Being there felt like a wonderful little gathering among friends - intimate and open. And then something would remind me that I was sitting right next to the leader of our state.

Cool conversation about the state of our state and our nation and other things of political interest. Totally enjoyed my time there. I had one of those moments, sitting next to Chris on the couch, of overwhelming pride. I peeked at him and smiled to myself, choked back some emotion, and looked around the room and almost had to pinch myself.

As we were standing up to leave the Governor asked me what I do...the million dollar question (I know some of you are laughing right now). Once again, how do I explain what I do? I laughed as usual and then told him. He had a priceless look on his face..."scrapbooking?" And then I said - are you ready for this - "I brought a magazine with me so I could show you just what I do. It is in the car." He had a big smile on his face and told me he would walk us out to the car so he could get the magazine.

You know I was loving it at that point.

We said goodbye as everyone was leaving and then he came out to our car, I grabbed the magazine. "Do you have a website?" he asked. Oh yes I do! I scribbled it on the inside of the magazine and flipped it to my article so he could see, really see, what I was talking about. A bit of joking ensued with Chris telling him how crazy (in a good way) it is this thing that I do.

God bless the Governor, he is such a kind, happy man. He has bright eyes and a keen takes a keen interest when you are chatting with him. He looked genuinely interested in checking it out, took the magazine in hand, said goodnight and walked back through the gate.

This is a happy-accident page. You see, originally I had put black chipboard letters down for the word "Gov," but when I looked at the page, I realized the letters were just too dark. While pulling them off, I discovered the letter backings were firmly attached to my paper. If I removed them, I'd rip up the paper behind the letters and would have to start a new layout. I decided to just go with the flow and leave the letters as is—and I really like how it turned out. It worked out just fine, and if I hadn't told you, you never would have known. Ah, glorious happy accidents.

A happy accident can also occur when you're creating a page and suddenly realize you need a supply you don't have on hand. For example, you're spelling a word and find you don't have the last letter to complete your title. Or, you run out of rub-ons just as you're about to finish your page.

I know it's easy to feel frustrated in that situation, but instead, remember this: Necessity can breed creativity.

Take the missing product in stride . . . and find a way to add in something else: a capital letter instead of a lowercase letter or a sticker in a different font. Sometimes I'll even cut up letter stickers and piece them together to create the letter I was missing. Try it.

... *and* **keep going**.

> Wanting to be prepared to take Simon on this grand adventure was on our minds a lot as the date grew closer. We wanted him to have an awesome time + not feel stressed, anxious, etc. We bought two books to help us all prepare and figure out some reasonable expectations about what it was going to be like in general — and then more specific stuff like which parks we wanted to go to when, etc. (+ food stuff). I was amazed at the amount of stuff out there just about getting ready to go to Disney World. I mapped out a basic plan for us — this park on Tues/this one on Wednesday but knew that we would want to be flexible too! Having Simon's story book made a HUGE difference for him ...I totally think it played a big part in how great the trip went.

★ ★ ★ ★ ★ ★ ★ **getting Ready** ★

Tuesday, 05 December 2006 at 02:39 PM

I have so many checklists going on around here right now. All those things I don't want to forget + all the class stuff for this weekend at The Scrapbook Shoppe. Shipped kits today. Packing my bags. Packing Simon's bags (Chris gets to pack his own). Picked up some special goodies for Simon's travel backpack.

And how cool is this? Simon's Autism Coordinator created this story book for his big trip. It goes through the whole process of going on the airplane, staying in his seat, eating snacks & playing with toys & watching videos, then seeing the characters, waiting in lines (got the doctor note), riding on trains, going swimming, etc. He loves reading it and I think he is finally getting it and he is really going. So cool.

Let's say there's a story you want to tell and you feel really passionate

about telling it, and then you realize you don't have a photo to go with the story. Time to panic? Time to discard the story? Time to move on to something else? Heck, no. Don't discard that story just because you don't have a photo to go along with it. No worries. There are many, many ways to tell a story, even without photos. Some pages simply might not have photos to illustrate a story or might benefit from the simplicity of the design minus the photos.

For some people, the idea of creating pages without photos is so beyond what they could ever think of as scrapbooking. But it is. It's telling your story. It's capturing your life through words. It's creating art with a few choice embellishments.

Creating layouts without photos can actually be very liberating. It forces you to think a bit outside the box and opens up a ton of possibilities for future stories without photos.

In the end, it's all about balance—balance between lots of words and a few words, lots of photos and a single photo, lots of embellishments and one or two. Be open to creative balance.

Today I am questioning.

Questioning myself, questioning my parenting skills, questioning my passions, questioning my sanity. All those tough, what is it really all about questions.

Real life questions.

Are we doing the best we can for Simon? Right now I feel like he is our of sorts. We are out of sorts. I am out of sorts. Getting shuffled around (*thank you God for Grandma Pati and Grandpa Al*) and missing school and missing the regular structure of a stable routine.

All that seems stable right now is instability.

I know this chaos is temporary. *I hope this chaos is temporary* and that we have not become so accustomed to living in chaos that we find that a nice stable routine is too "normal." Right now I am making changes and new choices to be home more, more available, more of what I think a good mom should be. Simon needs that structure. And then, a justification pops in my head: *change is ok.* It is part of life and we all need to know how to adapt to changes in our environment. And yet, Simon is different. In all those amazingly awesome ways he is different. And he is all that we know. Man, he is awesome. Positives and negatives. All about balance.

I am questioning. I want the best for Simon. I want him to be successful in whatever that will mean for him. I want him to be happy and have that feeling inside himself that he is a valuable human being. That he is loved tremendously by so many people. That he is awesome.

I know we can be doing more.

Life can be so complicated. Amazingly complicated. And then, at times, it all seems so very simple: love one another, care for one another, put family first. Do the right thing.

Do the right thing.

That is what I want to do. No more questions. Action. Make changes. Adjust schedules. Get done what I need to do so that he can thrive in that vital, amazingly glorious way that I believe - *that I know* - is possible.

Breathe.

Hold on. Change is coming. Change for the better.
JAN 2 9 2007

One of the things I've learned

through scrapbooking is that writing things down helps me deal with the stuff in my life. Without a doubt this has been one of the biggest benefits I never imagined would happen when I first began. It helps me sort things out and think things through.

I want my scrapbooking to be representative of my life. It's a combination of good and bad, stress and relief, positive and negative, defeat and triumph. I want the overall feeling of my books and projects to be one of gratitude, of hope, of appreciation for what we have. I believe we all have choices in our lives. We can choose how we approach the hard times and how we celebrate the good times. And we can scrapbook all of it.

I put this sort of layout right in with all my others— that's my choice. If you want to be more private, you can always set up an album just for you that documents the more emotional aspects of your life.

SIMPLIFY

DON'T
MAKE IT
MORE
COMPLICATED
THAN
IT NEEDS
TO
BE.

simplify

OVERALL, LIFE IS A PRETTY
COMPLICATED ADVENTURE. UPS AND
DOWNS. INS AND OUTS. DRAMA, EMOTION,
HEARTACHE, SUCCESS, LOVE, PASSION—
ALL ROLLED UP INTO ONE LIFE. YOUR
LIFE. GLORIOUS, ISN'T IT?

My goal with creativity has always been to keep things as uncomplicated as possible. Who needs another thing to complicate life?

A woman named Andrea recently called my work "active simplicity." I
like that. To me, that means there is life in my simplicity—something
deeper than you see on the surface, and I like that, too.

Scrapbookers tend to get caught up in the details, often second-
guessing themselves by asking questions like, "Is this the *right* color
of cardstock?" or "Am I telling this story in the *right* way?"

When I find myself getting too stressed out, asking myself too many
questions or taking too long on a project, I bring myself back to the
present moment by asking myself: Am I making things harder than
they have to be? Am I making things more complicated than they
need to be? I've discovered that I have the power within myself to
stop the stress and the fear and the questioning by bringing myself
back to my center. My center is the basics: the story and the photos.

In this chapter, you'll learn how to find your center and how to simplify
your creative process.

... find your
creative center.

Q: What is my creative center, and how can I find it?

Think back to when you were a child. Remember how instinctively creative you were? How you made stuff without fear of rejection? It wasn't necessarily good or bad, it just was. As we age, we become jaded and critical—especially of ourselves as creative people. We nitpick and sigh and get frustrated. And we're so very judgmental of ourselves.

That intuitive creativity you had as a child, with no fear of rejection and with no bias from the outside, came from your center.

Your creative center is the place where you begin your process—simply, it's the heart of the matter. It's the starting line, the take-off point, the place where ideas bubble up to the surface. For some of us, our creative center is inside our heart (based on feelings), and for others it may be inside our mind (which is more analytical). Most likely you experience a combination of both.

It's hard to explain how to get yourself there because you really already are there—*it exists within you*. The issue becomes how to tap into that part of yourself. That part of you that knows you are creative.

Each person has an individual voice that comes from his or her center.

For some people their creative center will speak first through words, for others it will express itself through photography, and still others through the use of techniques or embellishments.

It's easy to get away from your center, to be distracted from the heart of the matter. Stress, excess, time, professional and personal demands—all of these things make it tougher to align yourself so you're in tune with your creative center.

Take a couple of minutes to sit with this concept. Where do you begin when you create? What is the heart of the matter for you? Jot it down somewhere, and when you feel yourself drifting, when you feel yourself beginning to make things more complicated, reflect back on your notes. I have a small note on my bulletin board that simply states: Are you making it more complicated than it needs to be? It's a great everyday reminder for life and for art.

Are you a list-maker?

I have lists all over the place. Lists are a great
place to keep track of thoughts, ideas, things to
do, etc. Lists are a great way to stay organized.
They're also a terrific starting point for creating
life art. In fact, I'll bet you probably already have
a list somewhere that you could use as the basis
for a layout. How simple is that?

Lists have a way of making things less complicated. Sometimes I write out my journaling and read it back to myself and find my thoughts are way too jumbled. Breaking it down into a list format simplifies my points and gets me back on track—back to the heart of the matter.

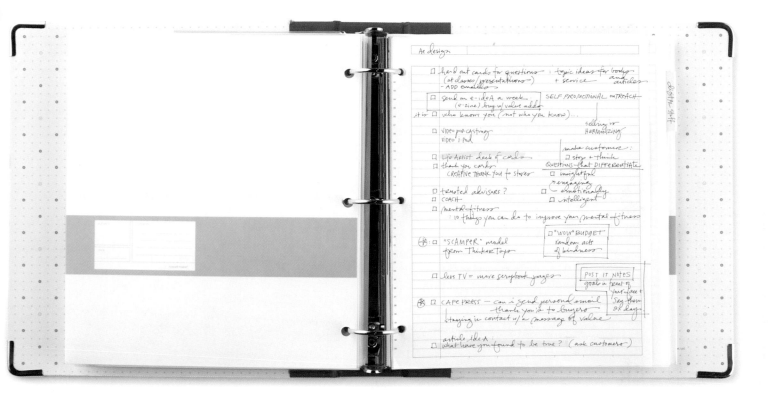

Life-Art Challenge:

Look for lists around your house and use one of them as the basis for a scrapbook page. If you don't have a written list, think about a story you want to tell and document it in a list format. Jot down the memories or the points of the story quickly in a list. Create a list of favorites, things to do, places to go, books to read, songs you love or anything else that appeals to you. Or, create a list of topics and stories you want to scrapbook. When you're feeling stuck, look at your list for creative inspiration. Simple and uncomplicated.

... *incorporate* creativity into your **daily** life.

BLANK

gratitudes for   FEB 2 2 2007 :

1. mom coming for a visit tonight.
2. Hot tea in the late afternoon.
3. my ability to stop what I am doing right now and go take a shower and then put on a cozy sweater + jeans.
4. clean fridge (+ a new one on the way)
5. having class kits for this weekend already shipped + arrived at their destination.
6. an email from Florence — thankful that I can have a friend on the other side of the world who brightens my day.
7. CHOICES. and freedom.
8. American Idol is on tonight.

Note to SELF:
do this more.
do this more.
do this more.
do this more.
do this more.
MORE.

THIS BELONGS TO:
me.
SO GIVE IT BACK

MINE MINE MINE MINE MINE

X NO LONGER BLANK

Q: *I feel like I struggle to find time to scrapbook. Sometimes finding time and getting all of my stuff ready for scrapbooking makes me feel exhausted. How can I simplify and find joy in the creative process?*

Living a creative life shouldn't feel like work. It should be something that makes your life better, something that energizes you instead of drains you. One of the best solutions I've found for keeping the process simple is to incorporate scrapbooking into my daily life—to do little tasks that get me farther along so when I have more time, I'll be ready to make the most of it.

I keep a file for stories on my computer, where I can quickly and easily jot down notes during the day. I add time to create to my daily routine, just like exercise, meal-planning or picking Simon up from school. And, I work in layers. Many of my projects, especially mini books, are built in layers. There are some days when I'll only paint a base coat on the cover of an album or add some rub-ons. Breaking tasks down into manageable chunks of time is a huge help.

Be realistic. We all choose what to do with the time we have. If you can allow yourself to be open to working just a little bit each day, you'll stay in touch with your process and keep your flow going.

Life-Art Challenge:

This week, simply add "creating" to your schedule. I know it may feel self-indulgent, but for a moment, think about how good it feels when you take care of yourself in other aspects of your life. Think of how good it feels to get a manicure or a massage. Think of how good it feels to watch a television show you love. And think of how personally satisfying it is to create beautiful things that tell your family's stories. This has the power to make a big difference in your life.

*... **accept** the creative cycle.*

rbcdelight

a new couch : a new love of life . all we can say is it is awesome.

our first piece of ADULT furniture. Lots of cuddling + napping now.

just an ordinary
SATURDAY in MAY 07.
It's a good thing we love our jobs...otherwise...big trouble. RBC = really big couch

We all experience a natural phenomenon called a creative cycle. Not a single one of us is immune. Essentially, it means we all go through high points and low points. Sometimes we feel super-creative, and other times we struggle to even pull out the supplies.

One of my biggest tips for making things less complicated is learning to accept this cycle of creativity. The simple truth is this: It comes and it goes.

There's a certain level of trust you need to develop with your personal creativity. Trust that it's taking a little vacation (or sometimes an extended one) and that it will come back. Living an authentically creative existence means being able to roll with the highs and the lows.

When I'm feeling "out of it" creatively, one of the first things I do is construct a very simple, solid page and force myself to be basic with the design.

Nothing complicated or fancy; simply tell the story. Sometimes ideas and additional inspiration begin to come to me. It's almost as if I need to let go of the desire to be creative before I can actually be creative.

This happened to me when I was creating the layout above. As I was about to adhere the photos, I begin to think about my stamps and looked around at all the bits and pieces of products I have in my studio. Bits and pieces are great story-tellers. Rather than tell my story through paragraphs (my initial intent), I decided to tell my story through products: stamps, stickers, rub-ons. As I worked through the process, allowing myself to begin with a solid foundation and go with the flow, everything started coming together, and I felt creatively satisfied with the result.

There's a whole category of foods out there that people refer to as comfort foods. They're the foods you reach for time and time again when you're sick, tired, wiped out, exhausted or heartbroken. Sometimes they're foods that remind you of home or of your childhood, and sometimes they're foods you know you can count on to soothe your emotions. They are comfort foods.

In other chapters, I've talked about how it's OK to repeat what works for you and about how you can find your flow and go with it by doing what works. In repetition and in doing what feels good, you can also tap into what I call "comfort

scrapbooking." It's recognizing that keeping it simple can include choosing a template, repeating it and maybe changing it up a bit to suit your mood at the time. It can feel wonderful to break your process of creating into simple steps, like cutting all of your paper to one size. Adhering all of the paper to your pages. Applying adhesive to the back of each photo. Adding an embellishment or two to your page.

The comfort in those simple actions can go a long way in boosting your creative confidence and helping you remember why you love this crazy hobby in the first place.

Life-Art Challenge:

Define what "comfort scrap-booking" means to you. Make a list of the creative steps you enjoy within a project. Make a list of projects that brought you great joy. Think about what components of each project were most satisfying to you. And then repeat as needed.

random advice #12
make your own tracks.

MONTH — *May*
DAY — *25*
YEAR — *2007*

It's so easy to fight creativity and to make it harder than it has to be.

Life art is about giving yourself permission to choose to welcome creativity and creative surprises into your life and your work.

One of my favorite ways to get re-energized is to allow myself to be surprised, delighted and inspired by someone or something. For example, I often surf the Internet for new ideas. I like to follow links from one to another—there's a ton of possibility in each click.

So much of the Internet is about sharing information. People share the things that fire them up, the things that inspire them, and the things that jump-start their creativity. With the Internet, you can begin surfing in one place and before you know it, you might land in a really cool place you never even knew existed (and it could be based on the other side of the globe). You might be surprised by what you find. Most likely, you'll learn something new. You might not even be able to wait another minute before you go and create something.

What's simple about being online? You can do all of this from the comfort of your own home or your own workspace. You can print out cool ideas. You can see different styles and designs and ideas, which may change the entire way you view the world—all by simply clicking.

Life-Art Challenge:

Go online. Begin with a friend's blog or a creative networking site (see the Resource section for a list of my favorites). Most people feature links on their websites that enable you to go from one site to another, following your own whims. One link will take you to another and another and another. (Make sure to take advantage of your browser's "bookmark" capability so you can reference the cool places you want to visit again. Most programs also allow you to set up files; you can even name one "creative browsing" or "inspiration.")

You're sure to find inspiration from people who are themselves inspired by what they love, by who they love and by what they do. Keep surfing until you find the link that inspires you to create something now. Other great sources of online inspiration: topical bulletin boards (explore scrapbooking boards, photography

boards, design boards, parenting boards), fashion websites, online auctions and more. It's really unlimited!

And here's the key: Make sure to set some sort of time limit for yourself. It's way too easy to get sucked into all the visual stimulation and then be too tired to create for yourself!

"I went to the woods because I wished to live deliberately, to front only the essential facts of life, and see if I could not learn what it had to teach, and not, when I came to die, discover that I had not lived." —Henry David Thoreau

In 2005, I took a good hard look at the holiday cards we'd received

throughout the season. Every December, I display them in our home (either in a basket, hanging by a ribbon or some other creative way), but after the holidays are over, I always encounter the same dilemma: I don't want to store all of those cards forever. In reality, who needs to keep all of those cards? (My mom would probably argue this point with me.)

My solution was to use my trusty square punch (a go-to supply for me on so many projects) to create a collage of photos and designs from the cards. Often, I can't get the entire family into the square of the small punch I'm using—and for me, that is OK. This page is a great example of taking an overwhelming amount of something (dozens of holiday cards) and narrowing it down to the essentials.

Choosing what's essential for you will always be a personal decision. My essentials are very likely different from what you deem essential. Sometimes it will mean using one photograph that speaks a thousand words. Sometimes it will mean journaling with just one sentence. But always, it will be simplifying. And that's a very freeing way to create.

celebrate the
everyday

TO ME, THE ORDINARY, EVERYDAY STORIES ARE WHAT ARE MOST BEAUTIFUL.

This is the heart of scrapbooking for me: capturing everyday photos and everyday stories. This is what I want to document. This is what I want to celebrate. This is what I want to remember.

This is the truth of our lives. The everyday ins and outs. The moments that make up our existence.

Everyday stories make our scrapbooks so much richer, with more documentation and detail and heart. They show a more complete picture of the lives we are living than simply a collection of birthdays and holidays would.

This can be a huge shift for people. It can be difficult to transition away from only scrapbooking events. It's a change in outlook, in attitude and in perspective.

But it's so worth it.

Everyday scrapbooking is really a philosophy in and of itself. It's a way of living. A way of looking at the world. For me, it's about documenting, chronicling, telling and celebrating life. That's what helps me understand and embrace the life I'm living. So much of it is about paying attention—opening your lives to the small details of everyday life. Cultivating a sense of gratitude for even the smallest thing—a smile, a giggle, the first hot sip of coffee, the way your child's foot peeks out from his covers each and every night.

And here's the best part: What I've found is that documenting my everyday has really led me to a deeper understanding of myself.

In this chapter, you'll learn how to do the same.

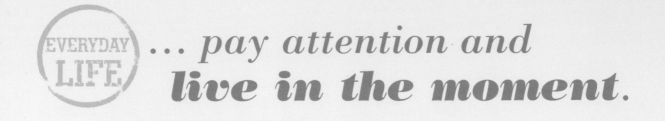

EVERYDAY LIFE

... pay attention and
live in the moment.

"Time, which is so often an enemy in life, can also become our ally if we see how a pale moment can lead to a glowing moment, and then to a moment of perfect transparency before dropping again to a moment of everyday simplicity." —Peter Brook

To be able to capture your everyday,
you have to begin paying attention to the life you're living right now. We live in a world that is go, go, go. You have to slow down enough to be both present and a witness to those awesome everyday moments. The more you pay attention in your life, the richer the stories you tell will be.

Live with intention. With your eyes open. Your heart open. Let go of all of the extra stuff that bogs you down.

These five tips will help you learn how to pay attention and stay in the moment:

1. **Keep your camera handy.** Remember, you'll miss all the shots you never take.

2. **Keep your eyes open.** Look at everyday things with a fresh perspective. See things again for the first time.

3. **Develop an observer mentality.** Become more aware of the daily world around you. Document conversations and the details of what you see as you go about your regular life.

4. **Draw connections over time** and look for patterns—patterns in the way you live from one day to the next, connections between generations (looks, habits, quirks), etc.

5. **Think about the basics** that make up your everyday existence: your morning or evening routine, the details of your bedroom or kitchen and more.

EVERYDAY LIFE ... scrapbook the **little things**.

Everyday scrapbooking is different than traditional scrapbooking. Traditional scrapbooking asks us to document the big moments of our lives, while everyday scrapbooking encourages us to look at details—the so called "little things." Little things can be the small bits and pieces, like paper, notes, cards, stories, a look or a touch.

And you know what I love about this? Each day I'm alive, I recognize more and more that it's the little stuff that is really and truly the *big* stuff. It's the morning routines and the bedtime stories and the nightly prayer and the daily battle to get to school that are really important to me. Those moments of daily life are a big part of what defines us as humans.

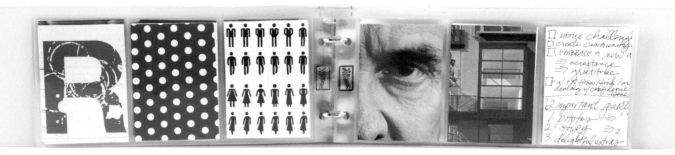

Any chance you have lots of stuff around your house? How about

extra photos, bits of paper and so forth (any chance you have piles like mo)? Here's a great project idea: Choose an album that has small page protectors inside and then go around your house and collect all the little stuff that represents your life.

For this album, I collected a random assortment of things: A couple of small pieces of a patterned paper I'm in love with. Part of a note I received from a friend. An extra copy of a photo I've already scrapbooked. A bit cut from a magazine or a cool quote.

Little visual treats like this inspire me. They make me happy. They inspire me both visually (I can get great ideas by looking at color and design) and emotionally.

And you know what? Sometimes I just don't feel like doing big stuff. Sometimes it's just a fun and a super-creative release to do something small and quick. No pressure. No big, long story. It's simply cutting out a small rectangle of patterned paper and sticking it in an album.

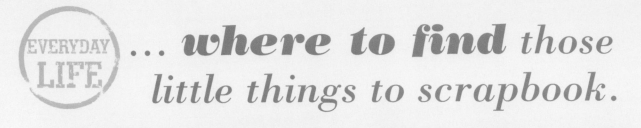

EVERYDAY LIFE *... **where to find** those little things to scrapbook.*

9.5.06

and you sang the ABC song while reading this book.

i love everyday.

toDay you

1 woke up at 7:05am on the nose and crawled into bed w/ us on my side 2 had eggs + toast + 2 bananas for breakfast 3 watched way too much TV while mama worked (but you enjoyed it.) 4 said "bye Andie. I love you." when I picked you up from visiting dad's office 5 had no nap.

Life-Art Challenge:

This week, set aside one day to practice looking for the details in your life. They're everywhere, just waiting to be found. Think of it as a treasure-hunting expedition, where the treasure you find is your own life. Take what you find and use it to create a piece of art that celebrates what you've discovered over the course of your day.

Q : How can I become a more detailed observer of the little things happening all around me?

It will take some practice at first, but you'll soon get the hang of it. Here are some starting points:

❶ Evidence of your existence. Take pictures of little things left behind by your spouse, your kids or even yourself, like shoes, coffee cups and toys.

❷ Possessions and collections. Books, magazines, craft supplies, kitchen goodies, flowers— take note of the things that have meaning to you (especially those things you love so much you make them a part of your home).

❸ Words and conversations. I have a series of albums called "Simon Says" that record many of the funny, serious and fantastic things my son says. Are there things you say all the time that are totally you?

❹ Signs around your town that relate to a story you want to tell. I actually have a whole collection on my computer of random signs waiting to be used on projects.

❺ Nooks and crannies. Take pictures of special spots in your home and of the places you love to visit.

... *capturing* the little things in photos.

Q : *I love the photographs you take. What makes you think, "Oh, I should capture that!" And do you have any tips on how to capture the little things?*

Such a good question. You really do have to think differently about capturing life than you may have in the past. You have to make a choice that these are the things you want to capture. I suggest making a list of the things you want to photograph in your home. Cross them off as you get the shot. I'll bet that taking these photos will open your eyes to all kinds of little details you would have otherwise missed. In general, I look for "the pieces of the whole" of my life—the tiny details that make my life unique. The holidays are a great time for capturing details, like the ones I share in this mini book.

Life-Art Challenge:

One of the best challenges I've come across for getting people into an everyday mentality is a photo-a-day challenge. I'm not sure when or where this concept started, but it's a great way to see things you would otherwise totally miss. It's an ambitious challenge, but it's telling and powerful and totally worth it. And, the photos make a great layout or mini book when you're done.

Pick a time frame and commit to take one single photo a day. (A week? A month? A year?) Try taking a photo a day during the holiday season and see what traditions and celebrations you can capture on film.

... everyday *details*.

"But the biggest mistake I made is the one that most of us make while doing this. I did not live in the moment enough. This is particularly clear now that the moment is gone, captured only in photographs. There is one picture of the three of them sitting in the grass on a quilt in the shadow of the swing set on a summer day, ages 6, 4, and 1. And I wish I could remember what we ate, and what we talked about, and how they sounded, and how they looked when they slept that night. I wish I had not been in a hurry to get on to the next things: dinner, bath, book, bed. I wish I had treasured the doing a little more and the getting it done a little less..."—From "On Being Mom" by Anna Quindlen

this week you were home from school on what they called a May break. Today was pretty reflective of the activities of this week - nice + relaxed.

memories TUESDAY may 21

today you

(love you buddy ... you are the best.)

9am: computer time while I did a bit of work. This week you have been all about the Big Big World on pbskids.org.

11am: we headed out to the Farmer's Market downtown. A bagel snack helped keep you occupied while I shopped.

2pm: just about nap time. You watched the movie Spirit (about horses) before we went and snuggled together for a nap.

5:30pm: Reading "If You Give a Mouse A Cookie." We picked it up today after the market. You love this book and must have read it 20 times today. The neighbor girls had just come and gone and you were back to the book.

07

Life-Art Challenge:

Choose a day and jot down notes and take photos of the basic elements of your existence. What time do you get up? What side of the bed do you sleep on? Do you brush your teeth before or after breakfast? Do you eat breakfast? Document all that everyday stuff you just do, maybe without even thinking about it.

Life-Art Challenge:
Take a break from reading for a moment and look around you. I bet there's something right in front of you (or maybe to your left or your right) that tells a story about your everyday. I bet there's some piece of paper near you that could become the basis for a layout. Did you find it? What can you create with it?

Check out the piles of stuff around your house. I bet you'll find things like receipts, notes, cards, bills, things that come home from your children's schools. Every day, I get so many random things in my mailbox. Some of them are perfect for creating projects that emphasize what our daily life is like right now, at this very moment in time.

... *look through* *the eyes of a child.*

Q: *How can I make my children part of my life-artist process?*

Do your kids have cameras yet? If not, you may want to consider buying an inexpensive digital camera for each of them. Kids are great at seeing what's right in front of them and capturing what they love. If you give them cameras to play with, you never know what wonderful focus they'll add to your life art. And, you'll get the added bonus of seeing their world through their eyes. What could be more enchanting than that?

My son, Simon, has autism.

He has taught me more than I could have ever imagined possible about living in the moment. About seeing things that most people miss without blinking an eye. About what is really important in our lives. Everything is a fantastic new adventure to him.

Because of him, I've learned to slow down and appreciate and celebrate the routines of our daily life. And because of his challenges, each of his successes feels that much sweeter. It's helped me take myself a lot less seriously. And that really is a wonderful thing.

Simon has taught me that the best moments are the everyday ones.

Life-Art Challenge:

Blogging is a wonderful way to capture your everyday stories. It's a great way to share and document your family's daily life. It's a great holding place for information and photographs. Many times, I copy and paste text directly from my blog onto a project or layout. My blog has helped increase my confidence as a writer. It's a daily practice. It's part of who I am. Consider starting your own blog. You don't have to make it public, and you can password-protect it. I encourage you to give it a try.

take a risk and ... play

PLAY IS A HUGE PART OF MY LIFE-ART MANIFESTO.

Play and risk encourage growth. They keep this whole creative process interesting and never stale. If you're finding you no longer love the creative process, it's probably time to shake things up a bit.

There are so many possibilities for play in capturing life and creating art. Some of it's in your attitude. Are you open? Are you willing to step outside your comfortable surroundings? Are you willing to take a risk to move yourself to the next level?

The type of risk I'm talking about doesn't even have to be something radical. It can simply be something like taking a different turn on your morning drive. Branching out and beginning your layout with patterned paper instead of cardstock. Turning off your computer and going for a walk.

Taking a risk in your regular process can have a huge impact on your projects and on you as a person. Take a vacation from thinking that things must be a certain way. Open yourself up to the possibilities. Nothing has to be the way you were taught it was supposed to be. Break some rules. Throw around some paint. Turn things upside down and around and around.

Ready, set, go. Let's play.

*... with **digital.***

Digital scrapbooking opens up a bunch of new doors for traditional artists. It can be as simple as adding computer journaling to your layouts or as complex as creating entire albums on your computer. What I love the most is the opportunity to combine the two (also known as hybrid scrapbooking). Here are some of my best tips for opening your mind to digital scrapbooking:

1. Don't be afraid of digital scrapbooking. It's simply another fabulous option for creating life art. In fact, it opens up a ton of new possibilities and avenues for you to stretch and grow.

2. Digital scrapbooking is not all or nothing. In fact, for me, it's a wonderful combination of the two.

3. Digital scrapbooking is just another way for people to tell their stories.

So maybe I have been a bit messy all along. I like to say that I am organized...and in my own way, I am. I like to make a mess and then clean it up and then make a mess again. It is part of my creative/organizational process. And in reality, the top desk is my Dad's...so maybe it runs in the family a bit. One of the things I love about the second photo is the autograph photo from the actor who played Darth Vader. Love that. Love that I made a huge mess to clean it all up. A part of me. I like to rearrange stuff, get a fresh perspective, a new feel. I was like that then and I am totally like that now.

JUST A BIT OF A MESS

What's digital on my "The Scoop" page? I put the photos and the

journaling (plus the patterned paper behind the journaling) together as a group in Adobe Photoshop and printed at home. After printing, I adhered the block onto the background patterned paper and added the black cardstock strips, the ribbon and the additional accents.

When I scrapbook digitally, I create the main content using my computer and add delicious extras from my stash of supplies. I love this sort of hybrid scrapbooking because you can do as much or as little on the computer as you'd like. It's a great tool for creating life art.

And, it's always a great option when I'm working with older photos that I've scanned into my computer. When I print on archival paper, I've suddenly given new life to photos that may have been forgotten or that may have deteriorated over time. Digitally, I can slow down their aging process just a bit and keep them around for more people to enjoy. So many good reasons to play digitally.

PLAY ... *with* **see-through** *elements.*

Lately I've been playing with see-through elements. There are

tons of see-through products on the market right now, including acrylic embellishments, transparencies, clear plastic embellishments and frames, and even good, old trusty page protectors.

I love things that reveal something else behind them—a hint of what's to come. Revealing layers of photos and words and colors and products. The two examples here are both 12" x 12" page protectors with 20 pockets; they were inspired by an album my friend, Elsie Flannigan, created for a class. Many other options are available with a variety of different pocket sizes. So many places to tuck bits and pieces of your life. So many possibilities for play.

Q: When you create see-through pages, what do you do on the back?

In the case of these pocket pages, I simply created another page and slipped in additional photos/patterned paper and embellishments back to back.

Another thing I did that's a bit different than when I normally work with page protectors is that I attached embellishments on the outside. Who says things only have to be on the inside? Attach brads, add flowers or chipboard letters, and enjoy having a bit of texture on the outside of your page.

These kinds of pocket pages are fabulous for documenting vacation photos or bits and pieces of ephemera you may have picked up along your journey, especially if you're like me and enjoy taking photos of objects and every-day-life scenes when you visit new places.

Not all play and risk has to be a crazy mess of paint and free-form, off-the-wall creativity. Many times, play simply involves figuring out how you're going to use all of your photos to tell a story.

There are many moments when I find myself simply unable to scrapbook just a couple of photos. One of the simplest ways is to get them all together and then just adhere them to cardstock in a very ordered way.

My tendency is to take horizontal photos—it's my go-to, the way I naturally look through the lens—but this would work for vertical photos as well. Here, I laid out my photos and then adhered and stapled the transparent frames on top of them. I used my old Singer sewing machine for the stitching. (This sewing machine originally belonged to my mom, who received it as a gift from my grandmother. There's something so cool about the history of this machine and the fact that I use something from my life history to create my life art!)

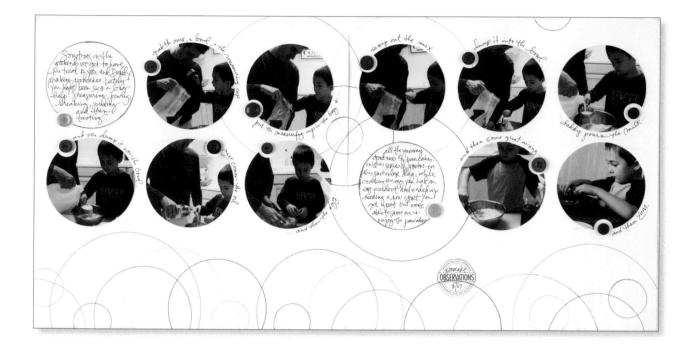

This is another example of the variety of page protectors available. This spread includes a page protector that's hinged with a seam. I used a circle cutter to cut the photos. Then I created a pattern with a variety of colored pens. One of my favorite techniques continues to be using a circle punch to remove part of a photo and placing an accent in the punched-out space. I love that. I do it over and over again, and it's perfectly OK.

While reading the Sunday newspaper one weekend, I came across this awesome "Amazing Grace" visual.
I cut it out immediately. I was so delighted to see something so cool as I read the paper and enjoyed my morning coffee.

Remember that life art is about living with your eyes open. You can find cool stuff everywhere—even in the newspaper that's dropped right on your doorstep every day. (I've found that Sunday papers tend to have the most interesting graphics and design ideas compared to other days of the week.)

I decided to use the "Amazing Grace" image as the cover for an album of current favorite photographs. Each photo is enlarged to the size of the album (8" x 8"). The interior follows a simple formula throughout, with the journaling beginning with "What I love."

To cover the clear acrylic album, (shown left) I used a gel medium. First, I dipped a brush into gel medium and brushed it onto the clear acrylic cover. I placed the image face down on the back side of the cover and used a brayer to eliminate any bubbles.

For the interior of the album, I started with seven photos. Then I selected seven different patterned papers, choosing the ones I was in love with at the moment. For consistency, I went with patterns that included blues (some have more blue, some have less blue). Each spread includes a small journaling block and three patterned papers punched into rectangles. You'll notice that this is one of my favorite mini-book formulas: Photos on one side of a spread and patterned paper and journaling on the other side of the spread.

I have a passion for photo enlargements. I love them. They often tend to speak for themselves through their subject, color and composition. They make an impact.

Over the last few years, with the increasing popularity of digital photography and online photo developing, enlargements have become more and more affordable.

This album contains a compilation of enlargements from different times Simon has spent with my parents at the beach. I love that it's something I can take out of its box and display on the mantel. I like to have my art where I can see it, and I enjoy rotating it around my home.

Here's how you can create this project:

1. Paint the interior and exterior of the box and the chipboard letters. Let dry.

2. Cut patterned paper to the size of the top of the box. Tear off a couple of inches of the paper. Adhere to the box.

3. Apply sealant (like a gel medium) over the entire box and the chipboard letters. Let dry.

4. Cut a transparency to the size of the top of the box. Adhere the transparency with large brads directly to the box.

5. Adhere round text rub-ons and chipboard letters to pages.

When I first started scrapbooking, I only created 12" x 12" pages. I loved the square size. I loved being able to fit so much on a layout. I never thought I would stray from this size. But the truth is, I started to get bored with only making 12" x 12" layouts. To re-energize myself, I started creating some 8½" x 11" pages and found that I liked that, too.

My dilemma came, though, when I wanted to put my layouts into albums. How could they all play nicely together in one album? I didn't want to have a bunch of different-sized albums or be limited by layout size when telling a story. My simple solution? I put both sizes into a 12" x 12" album. Voilà. Problem solved. I actually really like all the different sizes mixed in together.

Now I'm taking my page sizes one step further.

For example, why not add a layout that's 12" x 6"? No problem. I just trimmed a page protector to fit my page and slipped it in my album. (You can create a 12" x 6" layout digitally and then have it printed at an online photo developer. Check my "Favorites" index at the back of this book for links. Then, the photo becomes the base of your layout and you can layer additional elements over the top of it. That's what I did here.)

this is life.

LIVE IN THE MOMENT

a tall man + a small boy.
a fishing boat. a beach. a low tide. a
gathering of tools to dig clams. a woman
with a camera. a moment captured forever.

FEB - - 2007

"Inspiration weaves its way into every facet of life. We'd be sorely
remiss if we ought to be illuminated only by the medium or genre
in which we work." —Cameron Moll

In general, I'm not much of a "bling" girl. Never have been.

So to encourage myself to try something new, I reached for some bling and added it to my "A Tall Man and a Small Boy" layout on the opposite page. The result? I like it. It's different. It's very simple. Sometimes when you play, you'll love the result. Sometimes, not so much. And that's OK. It's all part of taking a risk and playing.

Another way to play is to combine something you do all the time with something completely different. On my "Chase Me" layout, I created a really loose artsy page and then added the photos in a very linear kind of way. I told myself to just begin. To not think too long or too hard. I was loose with my paint brush, and I allowed myself to change things up as I went. I asked myself questions like, "What can I add? How will this work? What can I layer on top?"

Life-Art Challenge:

Why not designate your next project as a play project? Collect lots of little leftovers from the products you've used on other projects. Mix up your embellishments by combining store-bought projects with bits and pieces punched from your child's school work. Add in newspaper clippings or a great visual from a magazine. Pull out your paint and just start without thinking too much about it. Grab a series of 10 or 12 photographs and figure out a unique way to display them. Put your work on a layout or take it to a mini book, a decorated box or a home-decor project. Do something you've never tried before. Play. Create. Have fun.

embrace
imperfection

LIFE IS TOO SHORT AND TOO AMAZING TO SPEND TIME WORRYING ABOUT PERFECTION.

The bottom line: Imperfection is reality.

This is the part of the book where I wish we were face to face so you could hear the tone in my voice and see the smile on my face as I say to you, "Get over it!"—whatever "it" may be for you. It's time to move past whatever "it" is that's keeping you from enjoying and creating and celebrating the everyday.

For some of you, "it" may be fear. Fear of making a mistake, fear of someone putting down your work, fear that there's a right and wrong and that yours will be wrong.

This fear can be paralyzing. It can stop you from creating entirely. It can cause you to sit and stare and get nothing accomplished for the two hours you have set aside as time to play.

What, really, are you afraid of?

Twenty years from now, your family isn't going to care the least about which patterned paper or embellishment or pen or cardstock color you used. They're going to be so very happy to simply have a little bit of documentation from you—a little bit of your heart that will live on. To know that you cared enough about them (and about yourself) to tell stories, to take photos and to do something that brought you (as well as them) joy.

You are a life artist. Tell your story—imperfections and all.

... *realize art is imperfect.*

"The answer is sacrifice. You have to give something up in order to get results that excite you and inspire the artist within. You must give up perfection. Perfectionism only provokes fear, and fear is what holds us back in pretty much everything in our lives." —Mike Colón

It's time to start embracing the fact that so much about creating art is imperfect.

I love to stamp. It's one of my favorite techniques. Stamping is inherently imperfect, and I think that's one of the reasons I love it. I love the extra bits of ink that jump onto my layouts, the messiness, the unpredictability, the risk, the humanness that comes out with each stamped image.

I also love to work with clear products, which tends to be pretty imperfect as well. Things are always getting messy and scratched. But you know what? It's all part of the process, a part of embracing all kinds of things in life. And the results are a fabulous representation and recognition of my own imperfections. Bring it on!

... *get over* fear.

aE&Kc

CRAVY

just a tad bit crazy... that is us. This is one of those people that INSPIRE me. She makes me want to create... maybe it is the fact that she is from New York and has that whole cool URBan thing happening...

whatever it is... she is just super fun + creative and can work transparencies like nobody's business So very cool.

05

06

My biggest creative fear is that I won't tell the story deeply enough.

Sometimes when I look back over my pages, I'm struck by how much I left out, how much more there is (or was) to tell, how much I wish I had focused more on the story and less on the embellishments and extras. I think this is one of the things that drives me to get those stories out as completely as possible, to the best of my ability at the time.

What is your biggest creative fear? You'll each have your own response to this question. Is it never getting caught up? Not being able to tell the story the "right" way? Not feeling artistic enough? Not having the right photos? Fear of criticism from friends or family or even yourself? Think about your answer (it might make a good scrapbook page!).

Here are some tips that will help you get over the fear that you need to create "perfect" stuff:

❶ **Recognize that "perfect" is a completely relative term.** We all have different definitions of the perfect house, the perfect relationship, the perfect way to spend time, and none of them is probably exactly the same.

❷ **Create for no one else but you.** This is a very liberating choice to make. (A benefit will be that others will have the opportunity to cherish it later on down the road.) It's OK to create only for you.

❸ **Force yourself to make something messy** (for some of you, this will be easy, and for others, it will be very difficult).

❹ **Use stuff that's inherently imperfect.** Think of those photo-booth photos you take just for fun. You know going into the booth that they aren't going to be perfect, and yet, they are the perfect snapshot of your life at that moment.

... *your family will love whatever you create.*

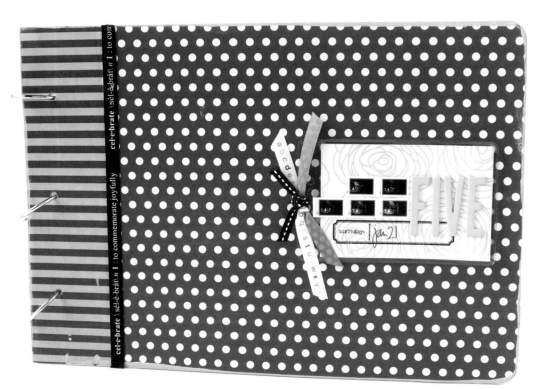

Let's chat a bit about perspective.

Perspective can really become your friend when you start to get frustrated with perfectionism. Simply remember this: Ten, twenty, thirty or more years from now, your family isn't going to care whether you decided to use a striped patterned paper or a floral patterned paper or the perfect color of green on your layout. Stop worrying about what anyone else is going to think and start enjoying yourself. This is a hobby that's as much about personal enjoyment as it is about preserving memories for the future.

This album is a great example. I created it to celebrate Simon's fifth birthday. I kept walking by it and thinking, "I need to add something more—it's just not enough." But Simon loves this album. He doesn't care if I add some stamps or some more embellishments. He's so happy to just open up the album and see the photos.

And I'm good with that. That keeps me going. And moving on to the next story.

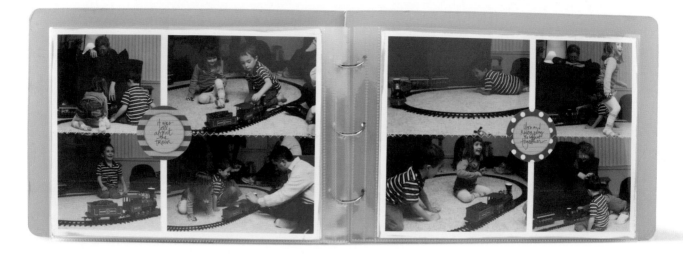

Life-Art Challenge:

Think about this concept in your own life. What items have you inherited from family members? Are they precious to you? Do you look at old photographs and think about how the photographer could have used better composition principles? Do you look at old books with handwritten inscriptions or crumbling baby books and wish your family member had selected a different style? I'll bet you don't. I'll bet you're just like Simon—happy to open up an album or book and see photographs and some sort of record, some sort of documentation. Create a project with this in mind.

... scrapbook on the road.

Scrapbooking on the road—what is it? It's a way to document your experiences as they're happening. You don't really have a chance to worry about perfection when you're traveling. You're on the go. You're busy. But the benefit of capturing your experiences while having them is invaluable.

I absolutely love making these books because they feel almost alive when I hold them in my hands. All of the bits and pieces from my trip feel like they're breathing.

I always bring a book with me on the road because my immediate reflections of a place are important to me. And I know I lose that sense of wonder and excitement (as well as the great little details) by the time I come home. Writing while I'm on the road keeps it all fresh. When I arrive

home, I can add photos and create other cool projects as well. The writing while you are on the trip is the key element. You're creating art while you're experiencing life.

You don't have to complete your album on the road, but it's a fantastic starting point. I completed this album almost a year after I took this trip because life and other stuff got in the way (sound familiar?) There is absolutely no way I would have remembered everything I included in my album without recording details as they happened.

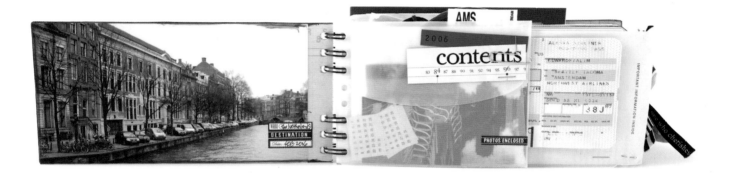

Want to try it? Here's what I suggest you take along with you. Remember, the goal isn't to pack like you're going to a crop party—stick with the basics.

- **An album** (Spiral albums are great because you can pull them apart and add pages as you go.)
- **A glue stick**
- **Scissors**
- **An archival-quality pen**
- I also like taking **one stamp and one small inkpad**.

Postcards make great add-ins to this type of album; journal on the back and add them to your book when you're back home. Or, simply glue them right into your book and journal on the opposite side. Look for other types of ephemera that will fit into your album as well, like labels, receipts, brochures, menus, business cards and more.

... *use* those
imperfect photos.

Most people take average photos. Wonderfully amazing average photos. I love average photos. They are real life.

My photos are delightfully imperfect. I love that there are blurry ones and off-color ones and off-center ones. I love that I can use all of them to tell my stories. I take average photos. Lots and lots and lots of average ones to get one or two that are amazing—that strike a chord so deep inside me that I have to yell to Chris to come and check it out on my computer.

In my own creative process, I've decided there are just a few things I want to focus on when I'm taking photos. I know very little about technical photography, and I'm OK with that. My brain is already so full of other information that this is one place I figure I can let go.

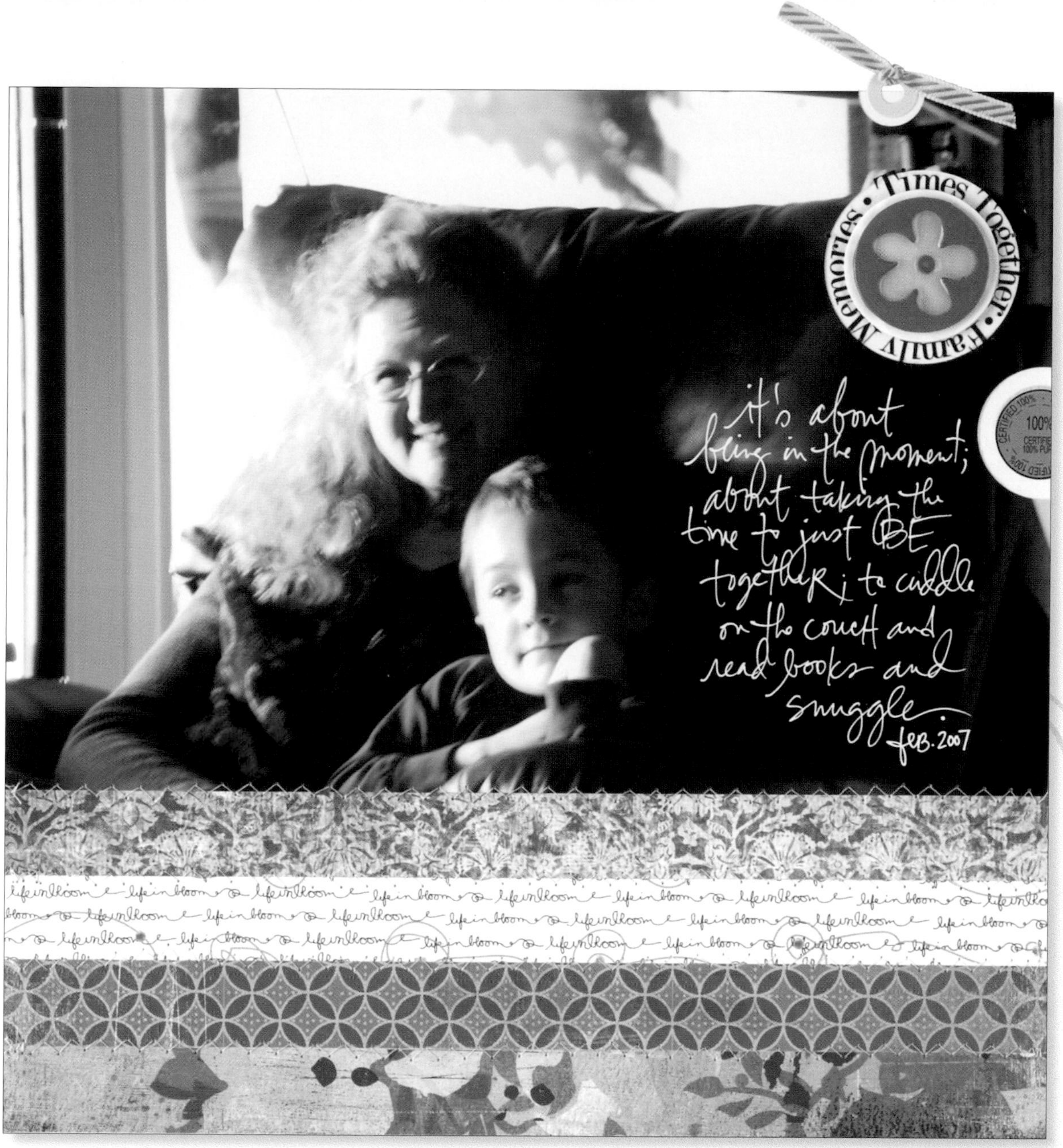

it's about being in the moment; about taking the time to just BE together; to cuddle on the couch and read books and snuggle. —Feb. 2007

Here are some of my favorite photo tips:

❶ **Get up close—and far away.** Give yourself options when it comes time to tell the story. Far-away shots show much more of the "life" in our lives, like the crazy color of your carpet or that mod lamp in the corner of your room.

❷ **Turn off your flash.** I love the absolute real quality that comes from flash-free photos. Sometimes they turn out a bit blurry; sometimes they're a bit orange. Still, they feel very real life to me.

❸ **Take hundreds of shots and then some more.** The more you take, the more you'll have to choose from. Don't feel burdened by having too many. The key is that when you upload your photos, you need to take time to delete (yes, I said delete) the ones you'll never need. You really don't need 100 versions of the same shot of your child on the swing. Remember, you'll take more photos tomorrow.

❹ **Stop worrying so much about making things "just right."** It will hold you back from capturing the photographs that will tell your story.

❺ **Make sure you are in your photos.** This requires turning the camera over to someone else or turning it on yourself with a tripod. You are a part of your life art—don't leave yourself out.

EMBRACE
IMPERFECTION

83

Our Story

NO SHIRT. NO SHOES. NO PROBLEM.

Old photos are awesome.

They are magic. They tell a story from their own particular point in time. I love the off colors and the unique croppings, but I especially love seeing the faces of the people in my family. I love the ones that show our everyday lives—the ones that show what our house looked like: the bedspreads, the dishes, the furniture that still lives in my parents' house, the styles that have come and gone and reappeared again.

Q: *How can I best deal with older photos?*

My favorite suggestion for dealing with older photos is to use a large square punch and create month- or year-at-a-glance pages, depending on how many photos you have. If you have a ton, you might want to create mini albums on topics that are important to you. Pick out a few photos and leave them full size, then crop all the others into squares using a large square punch. (Look for a square punch that's bigger than 2".)

I recommend scanning the original photos and working with the copies. File the originals away in archival boxes or more traditional photo albums.

... embrace *your life.*

MONDAY
TUESDAY

SORTA LIKE

halloween

WEDNESDAY
THURSDAY
FRIDAY
SATURDAY
SUNDAY

everyday is a good day for tigger.

Embracing the imperfections of

your own personal journey—your own life experience—will help you live a creative lifestyle. Living creatively is a choice. It's one you can make regardless of everything else.

There's something that happens once you let go and decide you're going to embrace imperfection. This doesn't mean that you'll just roll over and stop trying; it means that you start living with a certain level of acceptance.

As you create, think about how you can embrace the crazy things your kids do. Or the crazy things you do. What makes you unique? What defines your life at the moment? Part of being a life artist is embracing the lives we are living right now.

Q: *How do I embrace those layouts I don't exactly love?*

Let's face it, we all create pages we don't love. I know I do . . . sometimes my pages just don't work out how I'd envisioned them. Do I throw them all away? Do I rip them up and sulk? Nope. I put them in page protectors and put them away. It's OK not to love all your pages. Just don't get caught up in trying so hard to make them perfect that you never get anything else accomplished. And remember this: The page you like the least may be the one your daughter, your best friend, your grandchild or your dad loves the best. To them, that page is special because you took the time to create it.

FIND YOUR
VOICE

TELL YOUR
STORY

Celebrate the happiness that friends are always giving, make every day a holiday and celebrate just living!
—Amanda Bradley

find your **voice** *and tell your* **story**

FIRST AND FOREMOST, IT IS OK TO TELL YOUR OWN STORY.

No one else can tell your story quite like you can. You have first-hand knowledge. You have perspective. You have it inside of you. Your story is who you are.

I, like many of you, began this wonderful pursuit of creativity as a way to document my child's life. What I never expected was how much good telling my own story would be for me on a deeply personal level. It opened up a whole new world of expression. It's how I communicate who I am.

I believe that releasing your story out into the world—even if only onto a layout—is powerfully wonderful. You will grow in understanding of yourself if you're willing to take the risk, willing to tell your own story.

You can choose to express yourself in so many different ways. Your method might not be through words. You might prefer photos, paint or embellishments. Whatever way you decide for yourself is the right path. And you are allowed to change your mind.

This chapter is an invitation to make sure that *you* are in your albums. It's also a general invitation to create projects that document the real life you're living. You may be in the middle of a trauma or at the highest point you've ever been. Begin where you are. Begin now.

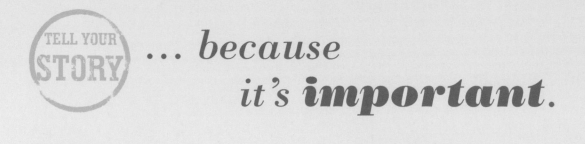

... because it's important.

Your story is important because you are important. Yes, you.

You, as the creator and the storyteller, need to have your life captured just as much as your subjects do. How many photos do you have of yourself? If you're like most people I've encountered during my travels, you probably have less than a handful of recent photos. Most likely you're always behind the camera.

Life art is not just about capturing others' lives; it's about capturing your own life and creating art from your own personal experience.

Why are you a scrapbooker? Why do you collect things? What do you want your scrapbooks to say about you? What is your story? The who, what, why, where, when and how of you?

My personal story is a mixture of so many different things. None of us is defined by a singular experience. We make so many different choices over the course of our lives, each leading us down one path or another. Each offering us an opportunity for growth and change.

And now you have an opportunity to begin making a change in your own life if you haven't been personally present in your work. This is not selfish—it's essential.

Life-Art Challenge:

Birth. Growth. Change. Ebb and flow. We all have a story. This type of album is your opportunity to tell yours, from the very beginning. Choose an album that can easily be divided into three sections, such as the beginning (baby/childhood), middle (college/early adulthood) and where you are now, wherever that might be. Scrapbook your own personal evolution. And remember, we are each built, layer upon layer, of memories and moments.

Remember
Today You

Here are my thoughts on the "rules" of storytelling:

Spelling and grammar and sentence structure are of the least importance to me. I was a literature major. I know the "rules." But here's the deal: I'm more interested in concentrating on telling the story, on getting it all out and down, than worrying about whether my punctuation is in the right spot.

All of that stress and worry slows you down and makes it much more complicated than it needs to be. And it can be a burden on the process of creativity. Let it go.

One of the things I share in my workshops is the idea that *it is OK* to let go of that high-school English teacher who lives in your head. The one who's always correcting your sentence structure, making sure you have a proper noun and verb in every sentence, reprimanding you when you don't follow the "rules." Maybe it's even time for you to have a short conversation with that teacher (*in your own mind, of course*). "Mr. or Mrs. So-and-So: Thank you for your time, but I am done with your services now."

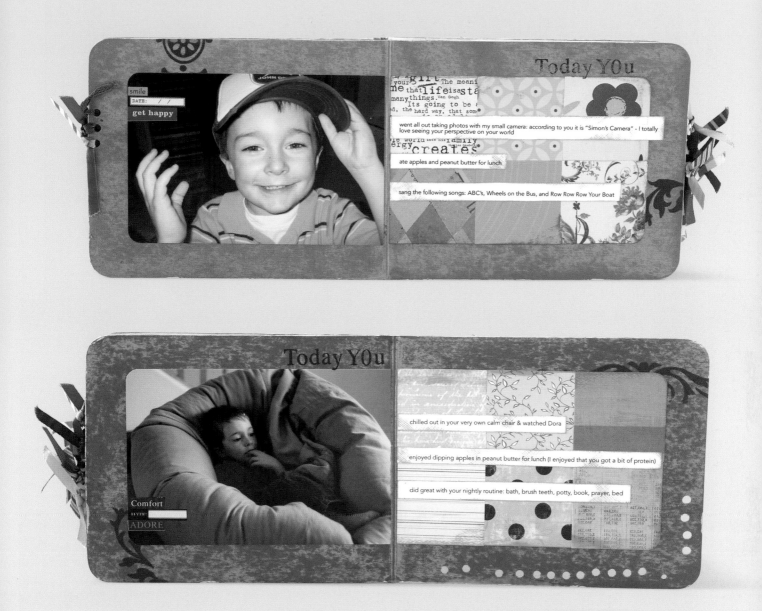

My love for words and stories is one of the reasons I was initially attracted to this hobby. I've always loved to read. I love to learn new things. I love to be taken away to another place and time simply by opening the pages of a book. It has only been over the last couple of years that I've come to enjoy writing almost as much as I love to read.

Part of the reason I've come to love writing is because I've been working on letting go of those voices that tell me I need to follow the "rules" when I tell a story. Now I rely on my own voice— these are my stories and my family's stories, and they deserve to be told in the most authentic way possible. And, I've realized that I can tell my stories in many ways. One word at a time. Or, as I did here, one sentence at a time. Your journaling should make you happy and fit what you're trying to say at the time.

When I journal, I try not to worry so much. Some of my layouts include incomplete sentences, misspelled words and other gigantic grammatical mistakes *(right now, those of you who are English teachers, editors, etc., may be cringing, but bear with me)*. I often like to journal in a stream-of-consciousness manner—especially when it's a story that really affects me emotionally. This means I'm writing more from my heart than from my head. *This is my voice.*

... with your
unique voice.

One of the biggest challenges in telling your own story has to be accepting and embracing your own unique voice. We each have an extraordinary ability within us to tell our story—as unique and individual as our fingerprints. The trick is trusting yourself enough to let it come out.

A breakthrough for me was giving myself permission to write like I talk. Writing like I talk infuses my personality into my written voice. I use certain words when I talk out loud—such as "cool"—so I add them into my journaling. It's more authentic and feels more "me" when I use words I say all the time.

Telling your own story doesn't have to be super-serious and earth shattering. It can be silly and fun. My ultimate goal is to be real. Not sugar-coated, not technical—just real.

Just be you.

THE POWER OF SONG

One of the most amazing things happened on Friday night at the crop - Chris, my Mom and I are still talking about it (*and I think we probably will be for a long time to come*). The big Friday night crop featured about 450 women (*and a couple men*) working away on projects, participating in the games, and just overall enjoying the company of one another (*and getting some layouts completed*). I was called up to the front to give away some prizes on the stage. I stood up there, said my name, etc and then Simon (*who had been in his stroller with Chris and my Mom*) came running up on stage.

He came right over to me and took the mic. Mikayla grabbed a chair so he could stand up tall at the podium. He babbled a few words all scrunched up together. I asked him if he wanted to sing a song and he thought a moment and began with the ABC song.

No fear. No trepidation. He missed the "L" which got a good giggle from the crowd. A big round of applause came at the end of the song.

But he was not done yet.

Next came "If You Are Happy And You Know It." The awesome crowd played right along as he sang the entire thing - including "clap your hands," "pat your knees," "stomp your feet," "beep your nose," and "shout hooray." People were clapping and stomping and beeping right along with him. It was awesome. I was totally amazed the whole time - the look on my face and my mom's face and Chris' face was probably almost as entertaining for people as listening to Simon sing.

He was confident. He was proud. He kept right on singing, finishing with a little song called "I love Mommy, I love Daddy." Seriously.

Afterwards he got down from the stage and ran around between the tables - no talking to the scrapbookers of course (saying "no" to people as they tried to give him a high-five). Up close is too personal for him but give him a microphone and an attendant audience of almost 500 people and he is amazing.

Sunday, 11 March 2007 at 10:52 AM | Permalink | Comments (111)

Here's **THE STORY**

Another journaling challenge is figuring out how to link our hearts and minds to help tell our stories more effectively. How do we achieve this balance?

We practice. We learn as we go. We keep this idea in the forefront of our minds—not allowing it to constrain us, but rather allowing it to free us to tell our stories without fear of trying to write perfectly. Remember our perspective: Twenty years from now, no one is going to be worrying about your grammar (*we all have more important things to worry about, don't you think?*). Instead they'll be thankful you took the time to actually write out your family's stories. Just think how often people come across old photographs of their friends and family and have *no idea* who the people are, let alone the stories of their lives.

...from a *visual perspective.*

LIVE IN THE MOMENT

I'm a visual learner.

I have to see things first and then write them down in order for them to stick with me. We all learn visually to some extent. I think one of the reasons I love life art is because of the visual-story-telling aspect. This also comes in handy with Simon. He does much better with pictures than he does with words. Looking through scrapbooks and other visual projects helps him understand his place in this world—his daily expectations as well as his relationships. I know things have become "clearer" for me since I started creating this way. I know myself better. I've found a way to express myself.

Make an Embossed Cover

To create the embossed cover on this album, choose a large stamp and wet it with embossing ink. (I'm a big fan of clear ink and clear powder.) After stamping onto the cover, dump thick embossing enamel (like Ultra-Thick Embossing Enamel by Ranger Industries) onto the wet ink. Use a heat gun to melt the crystals. Add the monogram accent and use the decorative brad to attach the plastic butterfly.

... even the imperfect ones.

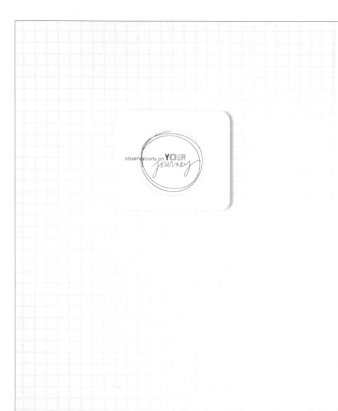

Sunday, 09 January 2005 at 09:04 PM

Last week, on Thursday, January 6th, Simon was diagnosed with autism. We had been on a waiting list for nearly six months for an appointment and evaluation at Child Development And Rehabilitation Center (CDRC). This is a division of Oregon Health Sciences University with an office at the University of Oregon. During our time at the center we met with a developmental pediatrician, a child psychologist, a speech pathologist, an occupational therapist, and a social worker. After testing (or attempting to test) Simon in a variety of areas the team met together to gather their findings.

Their findings were as follows: Probable Autism Spectrum Disorder with severe language delays, now echoing in Early Intervention supports; affection,

engagement, testing performance all pretty much on his terms, did not cooperate with standardized testing except for mild to minor delays, poor direction following; dislikes confinement or hand holding, little awareness of danger, lots of sorting, stacking, lining up, doors need to be closed, transitions difficult, lots of sensory issues, limited imaginative play

Hearing someone tell you that your child has autism is devastating. Even though we had some suspicions, by the time we finally had our appointment scheduled we had ruled it out...or pushed it out of our minds as a possible reason for many of Simon's delays. There are so many ways he does not seem autistic...and many ways that it is reasonable to understand why he is placed on the spectrum.

Thursday night we took Simon swimming. Everything was the same but everything was completely different at the same time. Our lives are forever altered in that one instant. Chris and I both cried as we fell asleep on Thursday night.

Friday morning I work up, and after dropping Simon off at school, headed to Border's and bought four books. I have almost finished 2 by this evening. Now I have a hunger for information...for what to do next. How to help Simon...how to arrange therapy...what direction to head.

One of the first things we are doing is putting him on a Gluten (wheat) Free/Casein (dairy) Free diet. To read more specifically why we are implementing this diet you can read the following: An Experimental Intervention For Autism. From the two books I read this weekend I am convinced that this is something that must be attempted first and foremost - and will occur in conjunction with behavioral and other types of therapies. We hope to be meeting with our Early Intervention connection this next week in order to move towards what is next...in addition to the speech therapy we have already scheduled prior to learning of the diagnosis.

So things will change around here. Pieces of our life will change.

Chris and I are good. We will stand in solidarity with Simon in this new diet. I imagine that my scrapbooking will take a backseat for some time as we journey down this road. There are so many things to be done...things to keep up with...to make sure that he is receiving the best possible care, therapy, and that we are doing everything in our power to initiate a recovery.

There is so much more to say I am sure and more autism links to be added. Thanks for the love that I know you are sending our way...it is so appreciated.

Not all stories are happy. And not all stories need to be told. Think about what you want someone

to know about you once you've passed on; by telling your own story, you have the power to choose now what you want to be told. What were your likes and dislikes, your greatest accomplishments, your passions, your favorite experiences, your challenges? I want my posterity to know the real me—and that includes some of the not-so-happy stuff in my life.

Telling even the not-so-happy stories is important because they make us real. They confirm our humanity. They link us to future generations (*and to the past*), because we all face challenges and disappointments. Can you imagine how cool it would be to read something one of your relatives wrote about the challenges (*and the triumphs*) she faced in her life? To know her true story? Not as a voyeur, but as someone seeking a connection.

Friday, 14 January 2005 at 01:23 PM.

In general I have always thought the following: you get sick, you go to the doctor, they check you out, they figure out what is wrong, they prescribe or suggest something to cure/fix/alieve/help. This does not seem to be the case with Autism.

With Autism it seems that we must become the experts. Then we get the fun job of going in to see doctors, watching their faces as we describe what we want done (say a blood test talked about in every autism book I have read so far)...and knowing that they think we must be crazy liberal wackos all into nature and stuff...handing over to them copied information and research, and on and on.

On top of dealing with this diagnosis we get to entertain (and attempt to educate) skeptic doctors with our talk of "leaky gut" and food intolerances and supplements and additional biomedical testing.
Basically it seems that we must become the doctor. We must learn all about what is being tried, what has been successful, and how to navigate a variety of medical fields. Sweet.

There is just so much to know...

All this came about as we met with an Allergist this morning. I went in with the idea that I wanted to have Simon tested for food allergies and for a few general ones (cat/dog, mold, mites - Chris is allergic to those). He has had a recurring stuffy and or runny nose on and off for a long time. We ended up doing the scratch test for the three - he was not allergic to any of them.

I told the Allergist what I have been reading regarding the effect of food intolerances/allergies on kids with autism. That through removing some of the common allergen foods some of the autistic symptoms could be alleviated. He wanted to know where I had read that - he had no knowledge of that - and gave me that "look" that I did not know what I was talking about. I had Lisa Lewis' Special Diets for Special Kids with me that includes an entire chapter on allergens and food intolerances. I handed it over and he read just a bit as we sat there and concluded that the basic premise made sense (must have made medical sense)...and that he had never thought of it within the context of autism. He photocopied the chapter.

After talking with him he recommended trying a dairy elimination diet (which we had already started last Sunday). It is possible that Simon's nose issues could be from a casein (dairy) intolerance as well. He also mentioned that the dark circles under Simon's eyes are another indication of a possible casein allergy. We have an appointment to meet with him again in three weeks to see how Simon is doing and revist our concerns. I plan to copy some more articles for him in the mean time.

The hardest thing for me is synthesizing all the information to present a cohesive case to the doctor. I get all jumbled up and intimidated by the MD after their name. In reality, I just need to remember that in most cases they simply do not have enough experience or knowledge about Autism. I need to be the one in the KNOW.

I struggled for a long time with the question, How could I (and should I) share Simon's life stories related to his autism?

I want Simon to know his history. To know what it was like when he was a little kid. At this point in his life, we don't know if he will live with us as an adult. There are more questions than answers. I don't want to present it in a way that focuses on the negatives, but I do want it to be real.

My answer was to create an "Observations on Your Journey" album. This album focuses on his successes and his challenges. But as you can see, in the logo I created, I changed the color between the "Y" and the "our" to emphasize that this is a journey that in many ways we are on together. It's a part of our shared life experience.

I look at it as a home for some information—information that's part of his personal story. We have lots of binders full of medical information for him; I considered adding some of that . . . but I decided to focus on the stories rather than detailed documentation.

... in a **series.**

Sometimes it's nice to tell a story in a series. This project includes

one box with 12 mini books inside. A bit of paint, paper, stickers and a stamp. One year of your favorite memories all in one great package. I love this project because you can do it all at one time—or you can create one book for each month of the year. Or, you can have each book represent a favorite moment in your life. Modify these little books in any way that makes you happy and helps you tell your story.

How to create these mini books:

① Buy a series of mini books.

② Cover the books with chipboard, cut to the size of each book. Round the outside corners of the chipboard covers.

③ Adhere the covers to the books.

④ Cut a piece of decorative book-binding tape to 2" for each book. Adhere to the spine of each book so that just a little bit folds over the front and the back.

⑤ Place a long rectangular-shaped label on the cover of each book. Write your title on the label. (It's a good idea to test your pen on an extra label first.)

⑥ Paint the edges of your books with the acrylic paint of your choice.

... *find words*
everywhere.

I mentioned earlier that I love magazines. They're a great source of design inspiration, and they're also a great source of words. It's fun to go through copies of old magazines and cut out words from headlines in different colors and font styles. Store your words in a folder or in a little index box, and the next time you need something unique on your layout, go and pull out a few of your favorites. Then group them together on your page in a way that contributes to the design of your story and the message you want to share.

We live in a world filled with words. As you tell your story, it's great to use your own handwritten words, but it's also fun to use other types of words. Look for printed materials you can include on your pages. For example, on a travel layout, it's great to incorporate words and images from maps, postcards and brochures. All of those things give a touch of authenticity to your layout and help you tell your story.

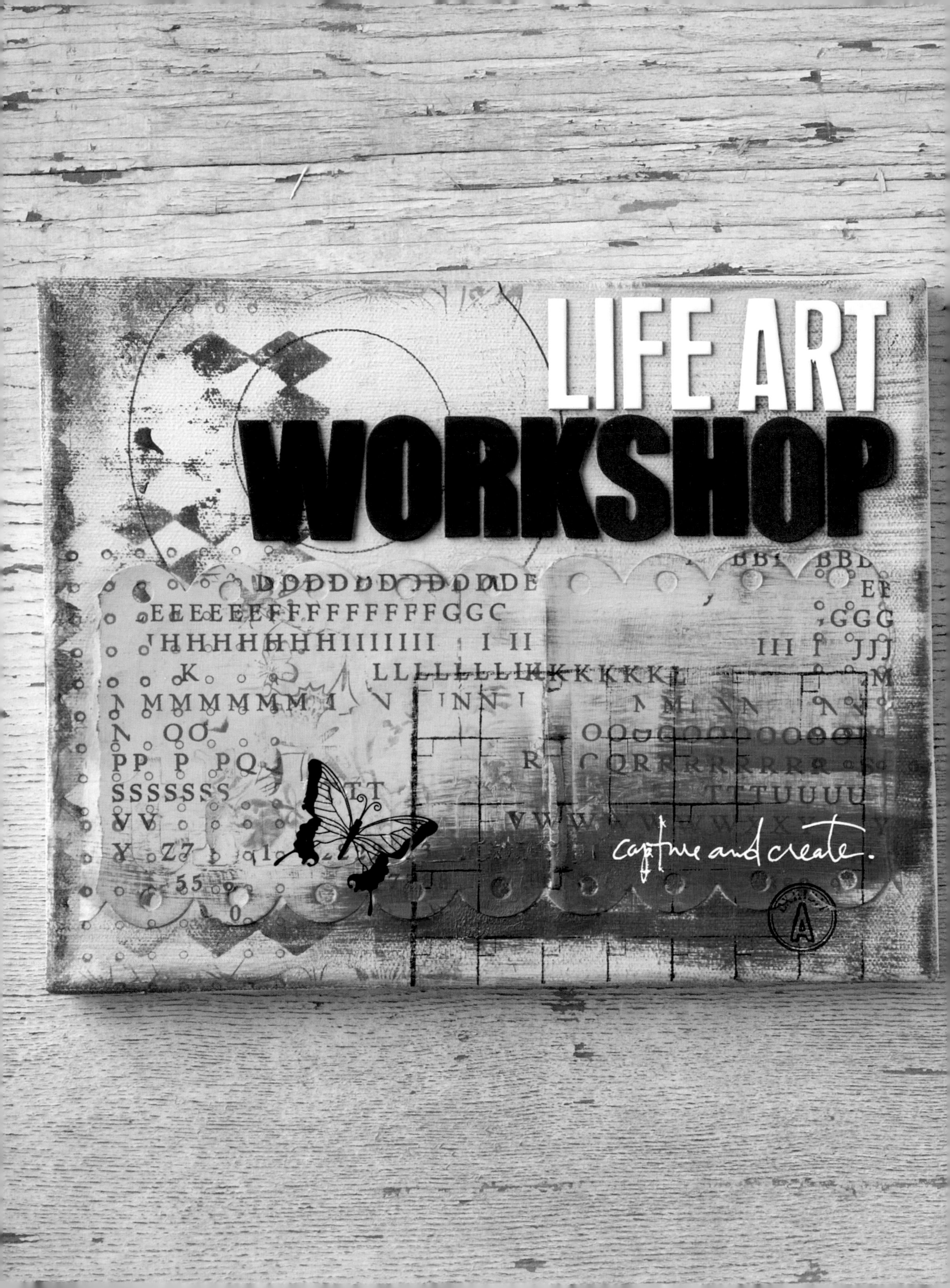
LIFE ART
WORKSHOP
capture and create.

life art workshop

THROUGHOUT THIS BOOK, I'VE INTRO-
DUCED YOU TO THE CORE CONCEPTS AND
PHILOSOPHIES OF LIFE ART. IT'S A WAY
OF LOOKING AT LIFE THAT EXTENDS
BEYOND WHAT YOU CREATE INTO YOUR
EVERYDAY EXISTENCE.

I'm a firm believer in the power of projects. I'm always coming up with new project ideas—some are doable within a certain time frame and some are totally far-fetched (gotta have these too). One of my favorite projects was a circle journal I participated in with a group of *Creating Keepsakes* Hall of Fame winners in 2003. That project moved me in so many ways. My creative world opened up as I saw and touched and experienced each of the projects as they came through my home. I got to wonder and ask questions and then learn from doing—which is what art is really all about. Doing.

In this final chapter, I'll introduce you to a few of my favorite projects. Take a look. Investigate. Even if you've never been to Disney World and never plan to make the trip, you can still come away with ideas from this album. Don't ever dismiss a project simply based on its theme. Keep your eyes open and take it all in.

disney album

In 2006, we took our first family trip to Disney World. Looking at my huge stack of photos after we returned home was overwhelming to say the least. My first question to myself:

What do I want to say?

As I went through the photos, the things that stood out to me most were the stories. The great everyday stories of our adventure. The emotional stories. The stories of the glances Chris and I shared over and over again as Simon's face showed his excitement and also, as he got tired, his frustration. I wanted to make sure there were words to go along with all of those photos.

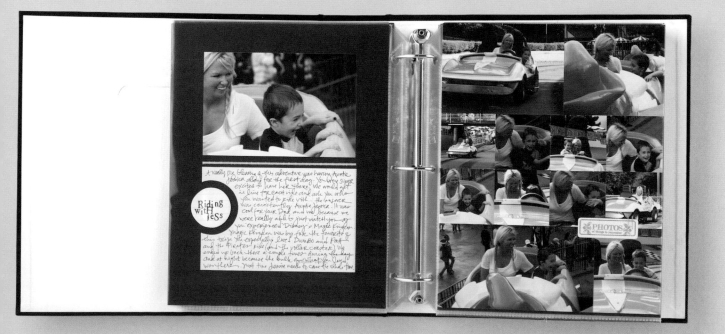

disney album

Tackling an album like this is a big investment in time and energy, so I came up with a system to keep things easy. Since I knew I'd have a lot of journaling, I had to choose between handwriting or computer-generating my journaling. Initially my plan was to type my journaling—this tends to be my choice when I have lots of stories to tell. But once I got into the actual production of the album, I found that handwriting was going to take less time in the long run.

I settled on an 8½" x 11" three-ringed album. One of the reasons I went with this album was that I quickly realized I was going to have more content than I could fit into a mini-book format. As for products, I chose just a few. I went with a couple of stamps, a couple of punches and some patterned paper. I've found that limiting myself makes the entire journey that much more enjoyable.

I also set up a workable structure for the flow of the album. I kept it basic since I knew the album would include several spreads, each with a favorite photo and journaling on one side, and a collage of photos on the opposite page.

My next step was to tackle the photos. I laid them all out on my dining room table. I needed a lot of room to be able to see all the stories I wanted to tell and to get them in some sort of workable order. I wanted the book to follow the same route as our trip: planning, arrival, park visits, etc.

If a certain memory or idea for a layout popped up while I was laying out the photos, I jotted it down on a sticky note and stuck it right on the photo so I wouldn't forget.

What quickly hit me again was that this was a huge project. Anyone who's been to Disney World and taken a camera knows that coming home to the prospect of telling this story is exciting but seriously a monstrous undertaking. I reminded myself to stick with the basics and focus on the photos and the story.

disney album

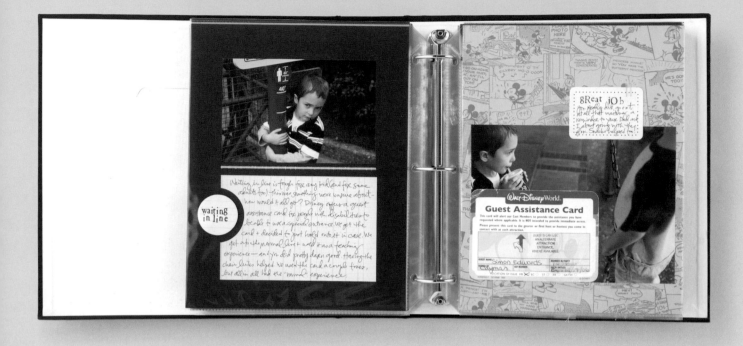

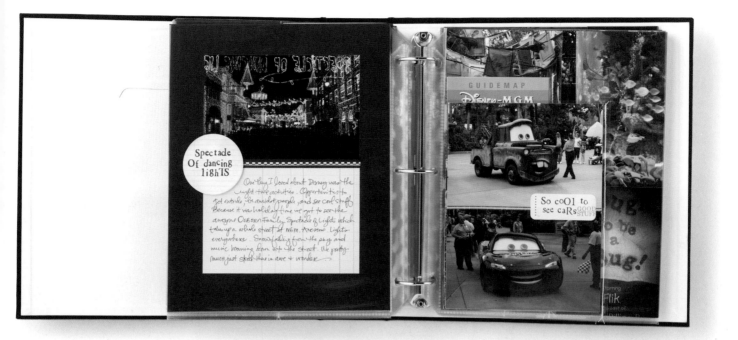

As you can tell by viewing this album, I didn't go the traditional route in terms of taking photos at all the specified "photo-op" spots. Instead of making sure I snapped all the photos I was "supposed" to get, I focused on capturing the experience—what Simon loved, his emotions, our time together as a family, etc. As a result, this album focuses on the things Simon loved most about Disney World: the train, the hotel, the stroller and the rides.

One of the coolest things I discovered as I worked on this album was that I could sew my own page pockets from page protectors. I simply stitched through a page protector to create one that would fit the photos/printed materials I wanted to slide in. I love mixing sizes and breaking up the "sameness" of things. Necessity breeds invention.

just begin
your journaling.

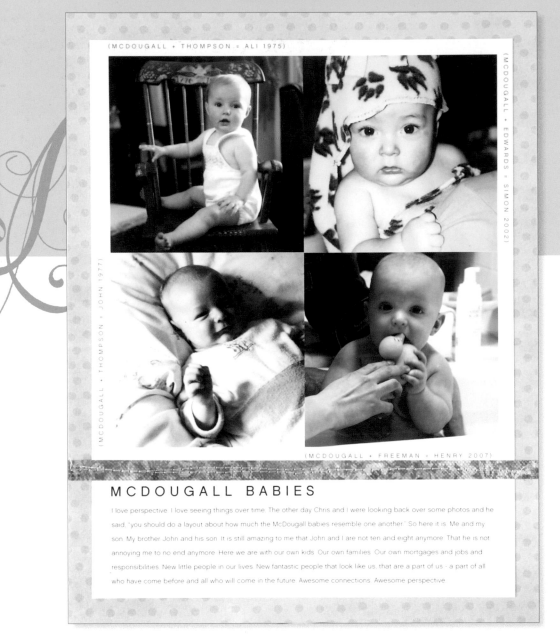

(MCDOUGALL + THOMPSON = ALI 1975)

(MCDOUGALL + EDWARDS = SIMON 2002)

(MCDOUGALL + THOMPSON = JOHN 1971)

(MCDOUGALL + FREEMAN = HENRY 2007)

MCDOUGALL BABIES

I love perspective. I love seeing things over time. The other day Chris and I were looking back over some photos and he said, "you should do a layout about how much the McDougall babies resemble one another." So here it is. Me and my son. My brother John and his son. It is still amazing to me that John and I are not ten and eight anymore. That he is not annoying me to no end anymore. Here we are with our own kids. Our own families. Our own mortgages and jobs and responsibilities. New little people in our lives. New fantastic people that look like us, that are a part of us - a part of all who have come before and all who will come in the future. Awesome connections. Awesome perspective.

Simply beginning takes courage.

To decide you are going to tell a life story is a big step for many people. It's a fantastic step. But it can be a challenge. If you're struggling with starting, ask yourself what's keeping you from going for it. Do you feel like you don't have enough time? Are you worried about the end result already? Are you just not in the mood?

The reality is that if you *just begin*, you will be on your way.

When that initial fear strikes me, I always try to come back to my center with the question: What is the story I want to tell? That is my simple six-word focus. If I feel myself getting off track (*and oh, man is that easy*), I bring it right back with those six words. I also usually ask myself: What will I want to remember 20 years from now? Or what do I wish I knew about my mom's life 20 years ago?

Life-Art Tips: Just Begin Writing

Let these tips help you get started telling your stories:

❶ **Stop procrastinating and just start writing.** I know what it feels like to stare at a blank piece of paper or a blank document on your computer. It can be paralyzing. Start simple. In the beginning, don't worry about going in the right order or what exactly you're going to say—just begin. You can do this.

❷ **Use single words.** Not all stories need paragraphs. Some stories can be told in single words or short phrases. I especially love using word stickers for this type of story.

❸ **Identify five stories you really want to tell.** Focus on those stories by pinpointing just a couple of stories in the beginning. Let go of that pressure to tell them all at once. And if five is too many for you, pick two. Don't spend too much time identifying what these stories are; pick two and get to work. Then pick two more. There will always be more stories to tell (*and this is a good thing*).

❹ **Keep a small notebook dedicated to stories.** Get one that fits in your bag—something you can keep with you so when you think of a story, you can jot it down immediately.

❺ **Stop stressing.** Stop worrying that what you write won't be "right." Embrace it. No one can tell your story better than you can. Don't create another page with the plan to add the journaling later (*I know you guys do this because you've told me in workshops*). Make a conscious choice that your words are just as important as the photos and embellishments.

week-in-the-life *album*

For the last few years, I've taught a class at Creating Keepsakes University called "A Week in the Life" (see more at *http://www.scrapbookevents.com*). This is an album that documents your everyday routine over the course of seven days in a row. It's a very detailed look at a specific time in your life.

This album is all about celebrating the everyday. The minutes and activities that make up a regular, ordinary week in your life. Washing the dishes, doing the laundry, your drive to work or your drive around town, the things you love to do (and those you're not so fond of), who you see, what you listen to, etc. Think of all the things you do over a seven-day period. Whether you're a professional, a stay-at-home mom or retired (or

something entirely different), there are so many things to celebrate in your everyday life—who you are, what you do and how you feel about your life as you're living right now.

As someone who loves history, I think it would be so cool to be able to read about an ordinary week in the life of someone I love from the past. What did she eat? What were her regular days like? Did she sleep a lot or a little? Did he have a job? Did he like his job? Did he watch TV? And if so, what were his favorite shows? These are the kind of ideas and expressions this album will document.

On the pages that follow, I'll share my ideas for collecting information and photos to create your own week-in-the-life album.

week-in-the-life album

The Basics

Keep track of these items for a week:

❶ Food. This one is simple . . . breakfast, lunch and dinner.

❷ Observations (three for each day). Keep your eyes open. What did you see today that you'd like to remember? What touched you? What did you notice that you haven't noticed before? This is where I included things as basic as, "The grocery store was super-crowded." Or, "Simon learned to jump." I also included things that were more about my feelings, whether I slept well, etc. Feel free to write more on additional sheets if you'd like. Don't forget to have your camera handy!

❸ Work. We all work in some form or another. What made up the bulk of your workday today? Running errands? A big meeting? Grocery shopping? Researching? Making calls? Detail what you worked on today. Feel free to include your personal feelings along with the details.

❹ Gratitude. I believe that cultivating a spirit of gratitude and thankfulness makes our lives fuller. Each day, I try to record the things I'm thankful for over the course of the last 24 hours. Most of the time, they're little things, like hot coffee. Record three to five things you're thankful for today.

Stuff

Collect this stuff for a week:

Collect and include *stuff* from your day for a week. Here are some of the things I included or that came to mind. *This is the stuff of life.*

- **Mail.** Return-address labels, covers from catalogs, notes from friends or family.

- **E-mail.** Print out some of the e-mail you receive during the week.

- **Ticket stubs.**

- **Receipts.**

- **Menus** or other marketing materials from a restaurant.

- A **magazine or online article** you've read.

- **To-do lists.** These are great representations of what you were doing on a particular day.

- **Newspapers.** Clip headlines, a comic you got a kick out of or an article that touched or enraged you.

Photos

Photos are an essential part of this album. I suggest keeping your camera at your side during the week (if you don't already). Think of yourself as a documentary photographer—look for shots that support the content you're gathering for your album.

Here are some ideas for photos to take during the week:

- **What you see every day.** Shampoo, dishes, your front door, the inside of your car, the inside of your refrigerator, your significant other, your child, your desk, the TV, your workplace, etc. I work from home, so I took quite a few photos around my house—the laundry room, my computer desk, my breakfast—documenting what it looked like during my week.

- **What you read.** What are you reading this week? Take a photo. Watch TV? Take a photo of the *TV Guide* or of the TV itself.

- **Places you go.** Snap some shots of street signs (just think how different these types of things will look 5, 10, 20 years from now). How about restaurants? The grocery store? Your church?

scrapbooking *inside* and ***outside*** *of the* **box**

The great thing about being a life

artist is that you can explore your art in different ways. As I've shown throughout this book, you don't have to scrapbook only on traditional pages. Here, I created a great little project that was designed to celebrate Simon's fifth birthday. The idea was to make something he could play with, something he could open and shut, and pull out and look through.

The construction is simple, and once again, it relies on just a few products to communicate the story.

I'm a big believer that the projects we create should be touched and read and loved. The mini books and small projects I've made have homes in baskets throughout my house. They're available for visitors to look through, for Simon or Chris to grab, or for me to take with me when I teach classes.

Don't be afraid of getting fingerprints on your photos. Share what you've created with those you love in a way that's easily accessible. Bring those projects out in the open and really live with your art.

To make this project:

❶ Attach the "5" to the exterior of the chip-board box.

❷ Paint the exterior of the box red. Let dry. Paint over the top of the red with brown. Let dry.

❸ Once the brown paint has dried, sand directly on top of the "5" and along the edges of the box. This will allow the red to show through.

❹ Cover the interior pieces of chipboard with patterned paper on one side and a photo on the other side.

❺ Adhere rub-on icons to the patterned-paper side, and rub-on letters to the photo side.

❻ Paint around the outside of the chipboard pieces. I used an Adirondack Paint Dabber by Ranger Industries—super-easy.

*your **creative manifesto***

In this book, I've introduced you to my personal creative manifesto. Each of these life-art tenets came about while I was teaching classes and traveling. These statements are things I found myself saying over and over again as I walked around the classroom. These are my personal truths related to my creative process.

Here's your chance to create your own.

grandpa&grandma

Henry's first Thanksgiving. The blessing of Grandparents. The delight of time spent at the new beach house on the Washington coast. Taking walks out in the fresh air. Baking cookies. Seeing the next generation grow. Listening to Simon call Henry "Harry" (and everyone joining in) and then telling him how he wants to show him a "tree in the backyard" (we later learned he was saying something about a "tea party in the backyard"). Happy hour. Lots of snacks. Cozy beds. Amazingly comfortable surroundings. I love that Mike & Kathy have adopted us into their family. One big family. Together. Watching all the kids grow. Such a blessing.

Be glad of life, because it gives you the chance to love and to work and to play and to look up at the stars.
Henry Van Dyke

Building Your Own Creative Manifesto

What is a manifesto? According to my handy-dandy computer dictionary, a manifesto is "a public declaration of policy and aims, especially one issued before an election by a political party or candidate." Essentially, it's a cool, fancy name for a mission statement—a way to describe your overall creative purpose.

Why develop a personal creative manifesto?

Because taking the time to define the creative person you want to be is a big part of actually *becoming* that person.

Because outlining your creative belief system gives you permission to grow and evolve as a life artist.

Because making lists is fun.

Because it's a part of your own life-artist journey.

Boiled down to its essence, a manifesto is simply a statement of beliefs. It shares what you stand for, what's important to you and what you aspire to be.

your *creative* **manifesto**

Here are some thoughts/ideas to consider as you begin building your own personal creative manifesto:

❶ Develop single words, short statements or entire paragraphs—any approach is totally appropriate. We're all at different places in our lives and in our creative journeys, and we all come to the table with different experiences and backgrounds. Your manifesto should be a direct reflection of you.

❷ Your creative manifesto can encompass your personal "truths," such as faith or simplicity, or be totally funky and light-hearted and fun (or a nice combination of the two). *You are your own audience, so tailor your manifesto to thoughts that resonate with and inspire you.*

❸ Recognize, as I mentioned above, that manifestos are constantly evolving. They change and grow and need to be updated over time. Whatever you decide upon now is not set in stone for life.

❹ Have fun with this. Don't take the process (or yourself) too seriously. Use this opportunity to define and establish your creative manifesto and the things that are important to you.

Life-Art Challenge:

The end of this book is really just the beginning. My hope is that through the journey of reading these pages you'll take away a new outlook on your art and potentially on yourself and your place in the world.

The final challenge is this: Create an album and title it "My Art." Dedicate this album to layouts and projects that celebrate you as a creative person. Maybe you'll create one layout a year or one a month (or just one, period). The idea is to construct a special, dedicated spot for celebrating you as an artist. Because you are. You are a life artist.

I want you to remember, as you work on your creative manifesto, that you are a creative person.

Yes, even you who's sitting there right now, shaking your head, ready to stop reading—you are creative.

As I've traveled around from store to store and event to event, I've noticed a lack of creative confidence in my students. Even those who are insanely talented and super-creative seem to dwell in self-doubt. Self-doubt is one of the biggest obstacles to creativity. It holds you back. It makes you question yourself and wonder, "Am I good enough?"

For some reason, scrapbookers have a tough time seeing themselves as artists. There seems to be a desire to downplay the inherent beauty in everyday artists—people who document their lives through words and photos. It's OK to be an artist, to call yourself an artist.

Remember, it is OK not to see yourself as an artist. But I'm going to invite you on this path with me anyway. I believe you are creative, that you are an artist, that you have a special gift to share with the world. That gift is your story.

Best friend to self-doubt is self-criticism. A bit of self-criticism is healthy and beneficial, and helps you grow and move forward in your creative processes. But when it begins to stifle you and hold you back and make you want to stop doing something you love, well then, it's gone too far.

Essentially, creative confidence is learning to trust your instincts. It's accepting that whatever you create has value and merit and goodness. This process takes time, but it's also a "right now" decision you can make. You can decide that you are, indeed, amazingly, wonderfully creative.

You are better than good enough.

... *more* challenges

One of my favorite ways to grow as a scrapbooker is to constantly challenge myself with new ways of thinking about my hobby. Sometimes the challenge can be as simple as rearranging the supplies on my desk or taking stock of what I currently love. Other times, I like to challenge myself to journal in a new way or try something new. The challenges on these pages will help you tap into all kinds of creative possibilities.

Life-Art Challenge:

One of the valuable things about looking over your past work is discovering what you really love and what you don't love about what you create. You have the opportunity to move forward with a focus on what's most important to you, whether it's the story, the artistic process or whatever.

Pull out a bunch of your old layouts and answer these questions: What do you like the best? What do you like the least? What works for you? What doesn't work for you? What things do you find yourself repeating over and over again? How can you embrace your imperfections and move on?

... **more** *challenges*

A great way to challenge yourself is to explore
using your supplies in new ways and in different
comfinations. A set of alphabet stamps can take on
new possibilities when comfined with other words
and images. Challenge yourself to come up with
creativie perspectives on what you already own.

Life-Art Challenge:

Think about the ways you might be making scrapbooking more complicated than it needs to be. Is it an issue of excess? Is it your confidence? Make a list of the ways you make things more complicated in your creative life. From there, choose one issue to address right now. How can you make little changes to simplify your process?

Life-Art Challenge:

One of the ways you can work toward accepting yourself as a creative person is to create layouts that celebrate the creative pieces of yourself. Take photos of yourself (set up a tripod) engaging in creative activities. Define, through words and photos, what makes you a creative person (and don't forget that creativity isn't limited to arts and crafts. Maybe you're creative in your home or in your garden or in your job—think globally). Tell the story of the creative part of yourself.

favorites

The Internet is a great place to find information and inspiration. Below you'll find a current list of my favorite websites to visit, as well as a list of books and magazines that inspire me. Remember that things have the potential to change pretty fast online, so forgive me if any of the links are broken.

To learn more about topics covered in this book and the life-artist lifestyle, visit my blog: www.aliedwards.typepad.com.

Blogs

Here's a list of my favorite blogs. These sites make me think, reach, understand, laugh and move forward. Often, clicking on just one of these sites will take you from one adventure to another—you just never know where you might end up.

52 Projects
http://www.52projects.com/

The Art + Life of Melanie Lyn Komisarski
http://www.navylane.com/musings/

Colorful Reconsiderations—I Love Life
www.lovelife.typepad.com

Hula Seventy
http://hulaseventy.blogspot.com/

Penelope Illustration
http://penelopeillustration.com/blog/

Sew Green
http://sewgreen.blogspot.com/

One of my favorite posts:
http://sewgreen.blogspot.com/2007/05/art-of-finding.html

Shim + Sons
http://shimandsons.typepad.com/

Shimelle Laine
http://www.shimelle.com/

Show and Tell
http://michelleward.typepad.com/michelleward/

Superhero Journal
http://www.superherodesigns.com/journal/

The Wish Jar
http://www.kerismith.com/blog/index.html

Online Challenges

Creative-challenge websites and blogs are everywhere these days just waiting to inspire you to try something new. Check these out:

Beyond Appearances
www.beyond-appearances.blogspot.com

The Dares
http://www.fortheloveofeffers.blogspot.com/

How Much Is Too Much?
www.hmitm.blogspot.com

Inspire Me Thursday
http://www.inspiremethursday.com/

Life Art Weekly Challenge
www.lifeartmedia.com

One Little Word
http://www.onelittleword.blogspot.com/

Random Challenge Generator
www.creatingkeepsakes.com/random_challenge/

Self-Portrait Challenge
http://selfportraitchallenge.net/

Studio Friday

http://tinesparkles.squarespace.com/welcome-to-studio-friday/

Two Peas in a Bucket

Check the message boards for a variety of different challenges.

www.twopeasinabucket.com

Websites

Here's an assortment of my favorite websites. These sites inspire me, educate me and motivate me:

Five and a Half

http://www.fiveandahalf.net/blog/from-prints-into-journals/

Flickr

http://www.flickr.com

Found Magazine

http://www.foundmagazine.com/

Inspiration Peak

http://www.inspirationpeak.com/

Mike Colón Photography

www.mikecolon.com

ScrapbookPictures.com

www.scrapbookpictures.com

The Visual Dictionary

http://www.thevisualdictionary.net/

We Are What We Do

http://www.wearewhatwedo.org/

You Are Beautiful

http://www.you-are-beautiful.com/STICKERS.htm

Books

I love to read. Here are just a few of my favorites that I refer to again and again:

52 Projects: Random Acts of Everyday Creativity by Jeffrey Yamaguchi

The Artist's Way by Julia Cameron

The Big Picture by Stacy Julian

Clean & Simple Scrapbooking by Cathy Zielske

Collage Discovery Workshop by Claudine Hellmuth

Computer Tricks for Scrapbookers by Jessica Sprague

The Creative Habit: Learn It and Use It for Life by Twyla Tharp

Design Basics Index by Jim Krause

Drawing from Life: The Journal as Art by Jennifer New

Everyday Matters by Danny Gregory

Living Out Loud by Keri Smith

Wide Open: Inspiration & Techniques for Art Journaling on the Edge by Randi Feuerhelm-Watts

Wreck This Journal by Keri Smith

Magazines

For me, big time inspiration comes in the form of visual stimulation. I turn to these magazines time and again:

Body + Soul

Blueprint

Country Home

Cottage Living

Domino

DWELL

HOW Magazine

Mary Engelbreit's Home Companion

supplies